DESPERATE DESERTS

AND

BLOOMIN' RAINFORESTS

Two Horrible Books in One

ANITA GANERI
MIKE PHILLIPS

SCHOLASTIC

Scholastic Children's Books,
Commonwealth House, 1-19 New Oxford Street
London WC1A 1NU, UK

A division of Scholastic Ltd
London ~ New York ~ Toronto ~ Sydney ~ Auckland
Mexico City ~ New Delhi ~ Hong Kong

Published in this edition by Scholastic Ltd, 2004
Cover illustration copyright © Mike Phillips, 2004

Desperate Deserts
First published in the UK by Scholastic Ltd, 2000
Text copyright © Anita Ganeri, 2000
Illustrations copyright © Mike Phillips, 2000

Bloomin' Rainforests
First published in the UK by Scholastic Ltd, 2001
Text copyright © Anita Ganeri, 2001
Illustrations copyright © Mike Phillips, 2001

ISBN 0 439 95896 2

Contents

DESPERATE DESERTS

Geography. What on Earth is it all about? Some geography teachers drone on and on about far-flung places you've never heard of, using lots of posh words even they can't spell. Is this what your horrible geography lessons are like?

TODAY'S LESSON IS ALL ABOUT AEOLIAN TRANSPORTATION* WE SHALL BEGIN IN THE KYZYL KUM...**

DID WE SKIP A PAGE?

* That's the posh way of saying a blast of wind. No, not that sort of wind. The sort that whips the sand up into sand dunes in the desert.
** Kye-zul-kum. Part of the Turkestan Desert in Central Asia. See what I mean about spelling?

WHAT IS SHE GOING ON ABOUT?

DUNNO. SOUNDS LIKE GIBBERISH* TO ME

*Careful! You're beginning to sound like a geography teacher. You've accidentally used a horribly technical desert word. A gibber is a stony desert plain. You'll be setting yourself homework next.

Luckily, not all geography is as desperate as this. Some bits are positively sizzling with excitement. Take deserts, for example. Don't listen to your gibbering geography teacher. Deserts are one of the most brilliant bits of geography ever. To find out exactly how brilliant, try this simple experiment to turn your bedroom into a desert.

Go into your bedroom and put all the lights on. Then turn the heating up full. This will make your room nice and bright and hot. Almost like a real desert. Then chuck a truckload or two of sand and gravel all over the floor. Plant a nice clump of palm trees (a few of your mum's best pot plants would do). And, if you're feeling really ambitious, get down to some digging and pile up some of the sand into a soaring sand dune. Congratulations! You've got your own desperate desert. Sort of. If your grown-ups start moaning like mad, smile sweetly and say you were only doing your geography homework. Then they can't complain. (On second thoughts, ask permission first.)

And that's what this book is all about.

HOW MUCH D'YOU THINK IT WOULD COST TO HIRE A CAMEL?

Hot enough to fry an egg, dry enough to drive you mad with thirst, and full of some very prickly characters, deserts are horribly hot potatoes. In *Desperate Deserts*, you can…

- fry your brains as temperatures reach 58°C.

- see the sun blotted out by a deadly duststorm.

- find out how to get water out of a frog.

- learn how to survive in the world's driest deserts with Sandy, ace explorer, and Camilla, her faithful ... camel.

This is geography like never before. But a word of warning before you read on. Go and fix yourself a good, long drink. Come to think of it, fix yourself a fridge full. Discovering the desperate deserts can be horribly thirsty work...

France, 1824

The young man with the mop of brown hair could not believe his eyes. Surely there must be some mistake. He read his newspaper again.

WANTED

Intrepid explorer. For expedition to Timbuktu. Must come back ALIVE. First prize: 10,000 francs. Apply to the Geographical Society of Paris.

It sent shivers down his spine.

The young man's name was René Caillié (1799–1838). He was far too skinny and frail to look like an intrepid explorer but that was precisely what he wanted to be. Never mind Paris, René wanted to see the world. One part of the world in particular. You see, for as long as René could remember, he'd dreamed of going to Timbuktu where the houses were said to be made of gold.

RENÉ CAILLIÉ

INTREPID EXPLORER

There was just one teeny problem. Tantalizing Timbuktu was in Africa. In the middle of the Sahara Desert in Africa, actually. Getting there was going to be horribly tricky.

René was born in La Rochelle, France, the son of a baker who liked to drink and ended up in prison. It wasn't a great start in life for the lad and worse was to come. What happened was this. René's father and mother died when he was young and he and his brother and sisters were brought up by his old granny. After leaving school, he went to work in a shoemaker's shop but he was always late or in trouble. His mind simply wasn't on the job. It was miles away … in Africa! On his days off, restless René shut himself in his room, staring dreamily at the dog-eared map of Africa pinned on the wall.

How he wished that he was there. Especially in the bits of Africa mysteriously labelled "desert" or "unknown". Every spare minute was spent with his nose in a book about travel and adventure. No wonder he was late for work. René was so busy reading books that he often forgot to go to bed. (Don't try this excuse at home.)

Now his dreams might just come true. The ad in the paper seemed to be written just for him. This was an opportunity not to be missed. The Geographical Society, too, had heard rumours of Timbuktu's fabulous gold and saw a chance for some serious money-making trade. Before anyone else found out about it. There was no time to lose. René grabbed his chance of a lifetime…

Various places in Africa, 1827–28

In April 1827, René finally set off for Timbuktu. Actually, he'd arrived in Africa some years earlier, with his granny's blessing. (Anything to stop him moping around the house, she said.) But he couldn't go anywhere without money. (Any money he'd had had been spent on getting to Africa.) So he got a job in a factory and saved up all his pay. In his spare time, he learned the local desert language and got into training by walking for miles and miles each day. Everything was almost ready. There was just one small (well, large-ish) hitch. You see, Europeans weren't actually allowed into Timbuktu, only Muslims. If René was caught, chances were he'd be killed. (And that would never do. In order to claim the Geographical Society's prize, he had to make a detailed account of everything he had seen and done in Timbuktu.) Did this put him off? No way! He'd come this far and wasn't about to give up now. Instead, René came up with a cunning plan. He'd disguise himself … as a Muslim, wearing long, flowing robes and a long, flowing headdress so that no one could see his face!

It was brilliant, though he said it himself! (He couldn't actually tell anyone else for fear they'd see through his disguise. Tricky!) He'd keep his notes hidden in a copy of the Qur'an, the Muslims' holy book. Then if anyone saw him reading his notes, he could always say he was praying. And in case anyone asked him why he had such a strange accent, he'd say he'd been kidnapped as a child and carted off to France. Now he was returning home to Egypt. OK, so it was a bit of a long shot.

On 19 April 1827, René finally set off with five local people, three slaves, a porter, a guide and the guide's wife. It was a dreadful journey. It was desperately hot and despite all the training René had done, his feet were torn to shreds. His path led through thick, fly-infested forests of grass, up steep mountain paths, through fast-moving streams and swampy bogs.

He lost his way three or four times a day and several times people almost saw through his disguise. But worse, much worse, was to come. In August, when he was about half-way, René fell desperately ill with a nearly fatal attack of fever. He felt rotten. And just as he was recovering from that, what happened? He collapsed with an abominable bout of scurvy, so bad that the skin peeled off his mouth. Yuk! He never could eat properly afterwards. (Note: scurvy is a horrible disease you get by not eating enough fresh fruit and veg – you have been warned!) Luckily, a kindly villager nursed him back to health with nourishing rice-water and herbs. (Sounds even worse than your school dinners.) And as soon as plucky René was better, he was back on his (still very sore) feet again. He spent the last bit of his journey travelling by canoe, down the Niger River, hidden under a mat so that no one would see his face.

Finally, on 20 April 1828, just as the sun was setting, brave René Caillié reached the desert and Timbuktu. At long, long last, his dreams had come true. Or had they? The books on Africa said that Timbuktu was so fabulously rich that not only were its streets paved with gold, but every house had a golden roof. Every day, it was said, caravans of camels arrived in the city, loaded down with yet more gold. Poor René had never been so bitterly disappointed in all of his miserable life. (Which just goes to show, you should never believe everything you read in books.) After everything he'd been through, the heat, the dust, the rice-water and herbs, he found himself in a city of "miserable houses made of mud",

where "not even the warbling of a bird could be heard."
(René's own words, not mine.) There wasn't a golden house
in sight.

WHO'S PINCHED ALL THE GOLD?

The Sahara Desert, Africa, 1828
But there was no time to lose feeling sorry for himself.
Getting to Timbuktu wasn't enough. To get his hands on the
10,000 franc prize, he had to get back home again – ALIVE!

NOW TO GET BACK AND
COLLECT MY PRIZE!

It was easier said than done. The only other explorer to reach
Timbuktu had been savagely strangled to death by his guide.
Would René live to tell the tale? It was going to be horribly
tough. You see, reckless René chose to return by a different
route. A route that led north, right across the desperate

Sahara Desert. It was a journey no European had ever tried before, let alone seen the end of. Things didn't start well. René very nearly missed the bus, er, camel. He had hitched a lift with a camel caravan which was going his way. But he was so busy saying goodbye to his new Timbuktu pals that his fellow travellers got fed up and left without him.

René had to run so fast to catch them up that he fainted. Luckily for him, someone picked him up and plonked him on his camel. Only another 1,600 kilometres to go...

For the next four months, René, his 400 companions, and their 1,400 camels travelled thirstily across the desperate desert sands. Woe betide anyone who fell asleep in the saddle. If you dropped off, you were left behind.

It was tough but rules were rules. The journey was worse, far worse, than anything René had suffered before. Day after

17

day, they trudged slowly across the seemingly endless sands and desolate rocky wastes. The glaring sun was terrible; the sandstorms were worse, blistering their lips and throat. The caravan was attacked by unfriendly locals. What's more, the food, if you could call it food, was absolutely foul – a mouldy mixture of flour and honey. (And to add insult to injury, René was nicknamed Camel Face because of his big nose.) But this was nothing compared to the throat-parching thirst. Camel Face, er, sorry, René, was thirsty all the time. It was like the worst type of torture. All day long, he could think of nothing but lovely, wet, dripping water. But lovely, wet, dripping water was strictly rationed to one drink a day and wells were few and far between. Many of them had run dry. Some of his companions were so desperate they bit their fingers to drink their own blood, or even drank their own urine. And when, finally, the caravan did make it to water, René had to fight off the camels to get a drink.

Eventually, utterly exhausted, burned to a crisp, with his clothes reduced to rags, René stumbled into Tangier in Morocco and went straight to the French Consul's house, expecting a warm welcome. Guess what? After all he'd been through, the Consul mistook ragged René for a beggar and kicked him out on the street. When finally he got back home to France, things began to look up for René. Not only was he given a hero's welcome, he was also awarded a medal, a generous pension and the Society's prize. But he'd had enough of exploring to last him a lifetime and gave up his travels for good. Instead he settled down and got married. And did he live happily ever after? Not quite. You see, not everyone believed his story. Some people said he'd made the whole thing up for the sake of the money. After all, he couldn't actually prove he'd been to Timbuktu. They only had his word for it. Who do you think was telling the truth?

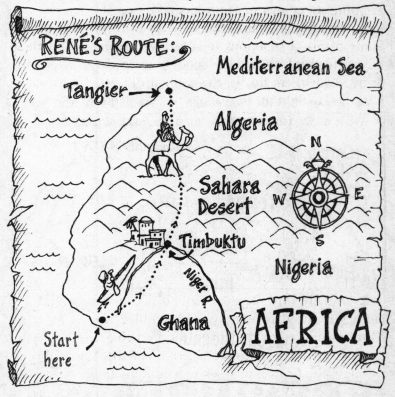

Desperate desert fact file

NAME: Sahara Desert

LOCATION: North Africa

SIZE: 9 million sq km

TEMPERATURE: Up to 45°C in the day; down to −7°C at night

RAINFALL: Less than 100 mm a year

DESERT TYPE: High Pressure (see page 30)

DESERT DATA:

• The biggest desert on Earth. It's as big as the USA (or Australia, with room to spare).

• In Arabic Sahara means desert. So you don't really need to say Sahara Desert, do you?

• About a fifth of the Sahara is covered in sand. The rest is rocky, pebbly and salty.

• About 6,000 years ago, it was green and wet with crocodiles, hippos, giraffes and elephants.

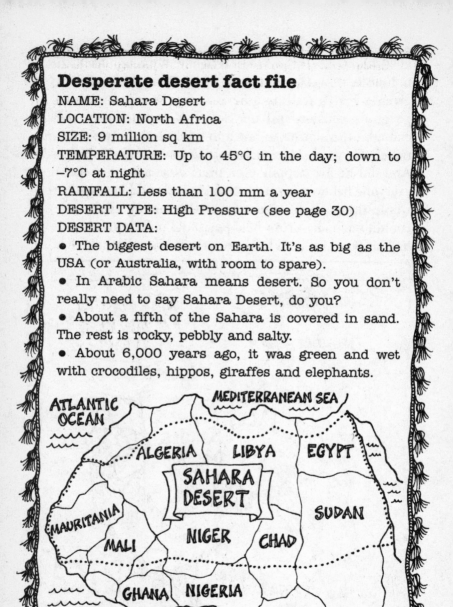

Sandy here. If you're thinking of following in René Caillié's footsteps and having your own adventure of a lifetime, you'd be in good company. Plenty of horrible geographers have had a go at exploring the desperate desert. Some of the lucky ones, like René, have even made it back alive. Could you stand the heat? Before you saddle up your camel and head off into the sunset, it might be an idea to dust up on your desperate desert know-how. (Don't worry, you'll have Camilla and me for company.) You never know, it could be a matter of life and death.

DON'T FORGET, I'M THE REAL EXPERT!

There might not be a desert near where you live but there's plenty of desperate desert around. In fact, deserts cover more than a third of the Earth's surface, and they're growing all the time. But what on Earth are deserts, and who on Earth gave them their desperate name? Horrible geographers can't agree (for a change). Some people blame the ancient Romans...

"DESERT" COMES FROM A LATIN WORD WHICH MEANS A DESERTED OR ABANDONED PLACE

Other people blame the ancient Egyptians...

"DESERT" COMES FROM AN EGYPTIAN WORD WHICH MEANS, GUESS WHAT? A DESERTED OR ABANDONED PLACE

Desperate, eh? Whoever thought of it first, the word desert stuck. (Thank goodness "abandoned place" didn't catch on. What a mouthful!) Though it's a mystery why the Romans had a word for a desert when they lived in the middle of Italy.

(Where there isn't a desert in sight.) The expert Egyptians, on the other hand, knew all about desperate deserts. They lived in the Sahara, which as you know, is the biggest desert on Earth. Not that they visited it very often. They thought the desert was full of demons and that anyone mad enough to go wandering off in it was likely to get their just deserts, sorry, desserts.

What on Earth are desperate deserts?

Warning – you'll need to use your imagination for this next bit. OK, here goes. Imagine you're walking along a sandy beach on a breezy day. (Put your fingers in your ears so you can't hear the sea.) It's the middle of summer and baking hot. There's no one else around. Your skin's starting to burn and your lips taste salty and dry. Your throat's so parched you can barely swallow. And when the wind blows, it flings stinging sand straight in your face. But more than anything else in the world, you're absolutely dying for a drink. Trouble is, there's nothing but sand for miles and miles. No water, no shelter, no ice-cream van. Desperate, eh? Welcome to the desert.

Hot and dry

There are two sure-fire ways of spotting that you're in a desert (if you hadn't already worked it out). Generally speaking, deserts are:

1 Baking hot

During the day, deserts can get desperately hot with temperatures well over 50°C. IN THE SHADE! (Yep, there's shade in the desert, if you can find it. Look out for a rare tree or bush, or a shady cave.) The ground's hot enough to fry an egg and toast your toes! The hottest temperature ever recorded on Earth was a sizzling 82°C in the Sahara. To get an idea of what this feels like, take the hottest summer's day you can think of. Now double it. Is that hot or what? At night, though, it's a different story. Because there aren't any clouds to trap the heat, temperatures can plummet well below freezing. Desert winters are even worse. Wrap up warm if you're planning a winter break in the Gobi Desert. You can expect teeth-chattering temperatures of –21°C and below. Brrr! Come to think of it, you'd probably be better off staying at home.

2 Bone dry

If you're off to the desert, leave your brolly behind. (On second thoughts, take it, it'll make a good sunshade.) It's extremely unlikely to rain. That's what makes a desert so desperate. Horrible geographers used to count deserts as places which got less than 250 millimetres of rain a year. That's about the height of the water you have in the bath, if you can remember where the bath is… Which sounds quite a lot but it's spread out over the whole of the desert. But now they've gone and changed their minds. (Geographers are always going and changing their minds.) Now they use a new-fangled system called an aridity index.

Aridity is the tricky technical term for dryness. But "dryness index" doesn't sound very impressive, eh? It's obviously much too tricky for some horrible geographers. They still stick to the millimetre method. Cowards!

Here's how the aridity index works. (Note: there are two different versions of this experiment. One's for a desert scientist with loads of high-tech equipment. The other's for you to try at home.)

See how dry a desert is – version 1
What a desert scientist would do:
a) Measure how much rain falls in a year in the desert (using high-tech equipment like rain gauges, radar and satellites).
b) Measure how much water evaporates (dries up) in the sun (using more high-tech equipment).
c) Divide **b)** by **a)**.

See how dry a desert is – version 2
If you can't get to a desert to do this experiment, don't worry. You can always try it at home.

What you do:
a) Count the number of cans of pop in your fridge, say two.
b) Then count how many friends you've got round who all want a drink, say eight.
c) Now, divide your friends by the number of cans to give an aridity index of four! $(8 \div 2 = 4)$

Congratulations! Your house is officially semi-desert. Count your lucky stars you don't live in the scorched Sahara. It scores an incredible TWO HUNDRED on the aridity index. Which means it loses 200 times more water than it gets. Talk about bone dry. But that's quite enough boring maths for now. Have a can of pop as a reward!

Desperate desert weather
Rain clouds? Where would we be without them? In the desperate desert, of course. Want to know why deserts are so deadly dry? It's because there aren't any rain clouds around. Sand and rocks, yes, palm trees, maybe, camels, probably. But rain clouds are extremely rare. Which, oddly enough, is what makes them so horribly important. To find out why, you first need to see how a rain cloud grows:

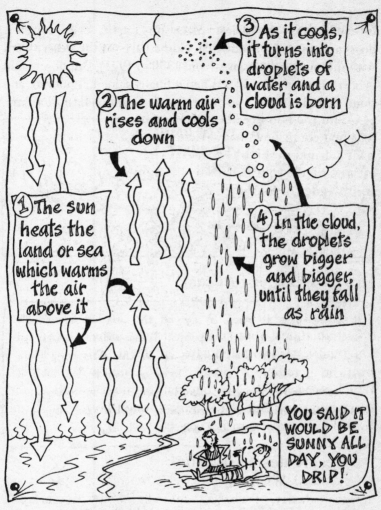

So why don't you get rainclouds in the desert? The trouble is that the warm air doesn't have a chance to cool down. It's so hot in the desert, it dries the air up. So rain droplets rarely form. Which is not to say that it never rains in the desert. Take the record-breaking Atacama Desert, for a start.

Officially, it's the driest place on Earth, even horrible geographers agree about that. Some parts of the desert went without rain for 400 years (from 1570 to 1971). But desert rain is horribly unpredictable. When it finally rained, it poured, and poured, and poured, causing chaos and furious flash flooding.

Desert weather forecast

It always pays to keep an eye on the weather. Here's the sort of thing you might expect... Today will start off hot and dry, with the wind getting up in the afternoon. There may be a chance of a dust storm or two if the wind is very strong. Expect cooler temperatures by evening.
Tomorrow will be much the same, and the next day, and the next day, and the next day...

You get very strong winds in the desperate desert because there's nothing to slow them down. They race over the ground, whipping up great choking clouds of dust.

And it doesn't stop there. Dust from the Sahara gets blown hundreds of kilometres, as far as the USA. Where it can fall in the rain and snow, turning them both bright red. Spooky! It must really get up people's noses. Especially as the Sahara's the dustiest desert on Earth, churning up 200 million tonnes of the stuff a year!

How on Earth do deserts happen?

Like geography teachers, desperate deserts are all horribly different. But they all have one thing in common – they're all desperately dusty and dry (a bit like geography teachers).

Any rain around simply passes them by. So how on Earth do deserts happen? Dip into Sandy's red-hot guide and find out about four different desert types.

Ⓐ Name: HIGH PRESSURE DESERT
Location: On either side of the equator
Aridity index: Very high
How they happen:

At the equator, warm air rises and blows away to the north and south. There the air cools down and sinks. How on Earth does this make a desert? Good question. Well, meteorologists (geographers who study the weather) call this high pressure because the sinking air pushes down on the Earth, putting the Earth under pressure. See? And high pressure brings sunny days and clear, cloudless skies. Sounds like perfect desert weather.

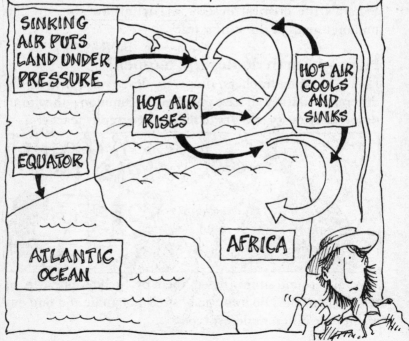

SINKING AIR PUTS LAND UNDER PRESSURE

HOT AIR COOLS AND SINKS

HOT AIR RISES

EQUATOR

ATLANTIC OCEAN

AFRICA

B Name: RAIN-SHADOW DESERT
Location: On the sheltered side of some mountain ranges

Aridity index: Very high

How they happen:

This is what happens when a mountain range gets in the air's way. As air rises up to get over the mountain tops, it cools down into droplets, and forms rain clouds. But by the time they've reached the other side of the mountains, they've dumped all their dampness as rain. So the spooky thing is that you can have desert on one side of the mountains and fabulous forest on the other.

RAIN CLOUD

RAINLESS CLOUD

MOIST AIR FROM SEA

RAIN SHADOW

DRY AIR

DESERT

© **Name: INLAND DESERT**
Location: In the middle of some continents
Aridity index: Very high
How they happen:

Usually, winds blowing across the sea carry masses of moisture for making rain clouds. But these inland deserts are so desperately far away from the sea, they don't stand a chance of rain. By the time the air's blown for thousands of kilometres, any clouds and rain are long, long gone.

D Name: COASTAL DESERT
Location: Off the western coast of some countries
Aridity index: Very high
How they happen:

Chilly currents flowing off the coast cool the air blowing inland. So it's much too dry to create a cloud. But fit some fog lamps on your camel. In the morning, the ground's still cold. It hasn't had a chance to warm up in the sun. In turn, it cools the air above it. Then the air condenses (turns into liquid water) and forms a thick, clammy blanket of ... fog. Bet that's the last thing you'd expect to find in a desert.

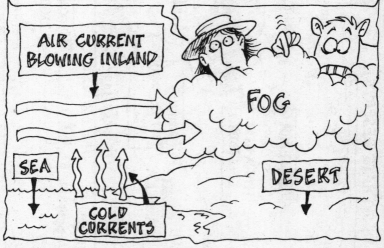

Desperate Deserts Top Ten

Over the page there's a handy map to show where on Earth the top ten deserts are and the type of desert you might just find yourself in.

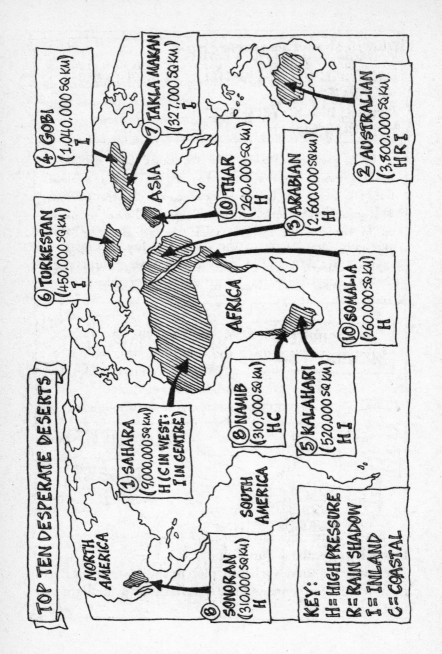

TOP TEN DESPERATE DESERTS

① SAHARA
(9,000,000 SQ KM)
H (C IN WEST; I IN CENTRE)

④ GOBI
(1,040,000 SQ KM)
I

⑦ TAKLA MAKAN
(327,000 SQ KM)
I

② AUSTRALIAN
(3,800,000 SQ KM)
H R I

⑥ TURKESTAN
(450,000 SQ KM)
I

⑩ THAR
(260,000 SQ KM)
H

③ ARABIAN
(2,600,000 SQ KM)
H

⑨ SOMALIA
(260,000 SQ KM)
H

⑧ NAMIB
(310,000 SQ KM)
H C

⑤ KALAHARI
(520,000 SQ KM)
H I

⑨ SONORAN
(310,000 SQ KM)
H

ASIA

AFRICA

NORTH
AMERICA

SOUTH
AMERICA

KEY:
H = HIGH PRESSURE
R = RAIN SHADOW
I = INLAND
C = COASTAL

Dying for a drink

Faced with all the things desperate deserts can throw at you – the horrible heat, the dust, the fog, it's a wonder anyone goes there at all. Or comes out alive. You need to be tough to survive in the desert. As this terrible true story shows. Picture the scene…

The Sonoran Desert, USA, August 1905

Dawn was breaking over the desert. It was going to be another desperately hot day. Scientist, William J. McGee lay fast asleep on the ground. A lizard strolled lazily across his leg and somewhere in the distance a hungry coyote howled.

William shifted slightly in his sleep but he didn't wake up. He'd been in the desert for three long months, studying desert weather and wildlife. Compared to the deadly creatures he'd seen, lizards were, well, er, pussy cats. Besides, he was having a very strange dream. In it, a herd of huge cows was galloping towards him, closer and closer, raising clouds of dust with their hooves. Suddenly, one cow let out an ear-splitting ROOAAARRR!

This time, William woke up with a start.

"What the…? Where's…? Who's the…? Mummy!" he mumbled, looking around blearily and reaching for his gun.

Of course, there wasn't a cow to be seen anywhere. Then William realized what it was he'd heard. He hadn't dreamed the scream – it was real. And whoever had made it wasn't far away. And desperately needed his help. Wide awake now, William scrambled to his feet and peered over the edge of the nearby cliffside. A dreadful sight met his eyes. A man lay on the ground. He was barely alive, his body a bag of bones. There was no time to spare. If he didn't have a drink soon, he'd die. William sloshed water over the man and gave him a sip of whiskey to drink. (Desperate times called for desperate measures.)

Then, slowly and painfully, through parched lips, the man began to tell William his story:

"My name is Pablo Valencia," he gasped. "My friend and I came to the desert to look for gold. There's an old gold mine we heard of and we wanted to make some money. We knew that summer wasn't the best time to come but we thought what the heck, we'll be OK. Anyway, somehow we got split up. My friend had our horses and supplies. I was left stranded and alone with only a canteen of water to drink. It was desperate. I tried to get back to the waterhole. I knew it must be nearby. But the heat was so terrible, it played tricks on my mind and I couldn't find the way.

At the end of the first day, my water ran out. It was terrible. I was so thirsty, I can't tell you how thirsty. It was like I was being tortured. I tried chewing on some twigs. I even ate some spiders and flies. But they just made me sick. At night, some vultures flew overhead, waiting for me to die. It seemed to go on for ever. I don't know how long it was. All I know is that soon I couldn't hear or focus my eyes. I couldn't speak or swallow. I was so weak I could hardly move. But I had to carry on. What else could I do? I crawled along for a while, but I knew that it was over. I said my prayers and I lay down to die. It was then that you heard me scream. It was one last desperate plea for help."

Plucky Pablo had had a lucky escape. He'd spent seven long, desperate days lost in the desert. If William hadn't found him when he did, he'd have died of thirst for sure. In fact, he went on to make a full recovery. But how on Earth did he survive for so long without water? What do you think he drank to save his life? Was it...

CAMEL PEE   HIS OWN PEE   HIS BLOOD

Answer: b) And he wasn't the first. Like many desert travellers before him, Pablo drank his own pee in a last-ditch attempt to quench his thirst. People have also tried drinking camel pee, blood (their own and their camels') and even petrol. DO NOT TRY ANY OF THESE AT HOME.

Teacher teaser

If you are dying for a drink but there's still an hour to go before lunch, try sucking up to your teacher with a spot of ancient Greek. Put your hand up and say:

PLEASE, SIR, MAY I BE EXCUSED? I'M FEELING A BIT EUDIPSIC

He'll be so gobsmacked, he's bound to let you go. But what on Earth are you talking about?

Answer: Eudipsic (you-dip-sick) is the technical word for being thirsty. If you're a serious show-off, you could always try hyperdipsic (high-per-dip-sick) for being very thirsty and polydipsic (polly-dip-sick) for being so desperately thirsty you'd drink anything (even camel pee?).

Horrible Health Warning

In the desperate desert, you can die of thirst. Literally. Without any water, you'll be dead in two days. Tops. First, you'll lose loads of water as sweat. You'll feel weak and your skin will get dry and wrinkly. Next you'll feel feverish and confused. Your blood quickly gets too thick for your heart to pump, followed swiftly by delirium and death. Nasty. To stay alive, drink at least nine litres of water a day. (That's the same as 27 cans of fizzy drink. Burp!) Even if you don't feel at all thirsty. But drink it in sips. Don't gulp it down. Otherwise you'll be horribly sick and waste the water. How can you tell if you're dehydrated? Look at the colour of your pee. It's normally a lightish yellow in colour. But if it goes darker, you're in trouble. Have something to drink immediately.

Still desperate to go? Well, you have been warned. And don't forget, if you're determined to trek through the deadly desert, take as much water with you as you can carry. You never know when you'll find the next welcoming well or waterhole. Besides, you're going to need all the refreshments you can get to help you through the next choking chapter. It's all about bone-dry sand.

SHIFTING SANDS

So far, all the deserts you've come across have been full of miles and miles of baking hot sand, with a scattering of palm trees and camels. Exactly what you'd expect a desert to look like. But deserts aren't always quite like that. In fact, only a quarter are sandy at all. (Tell that to your teacher.) Most are made up of miles of rolling, rocky plains, covered in piles of pebbles and gravel. A few have mountains in the middle. (They're all that's left of violent volcanoes. Don't worry, it's been millions of years since these freaky peaks last blew their tops.) But if it's sand you want...

Seven sizzling facts about sand

1 Never ask a horrible geographer a simple question, unless you've got plenty of time on your hands. Take "What on Earth is sand?", for example. A geography expert will waffle on and on about aeolian (ay-ow-lee-an) lowering until you fall asleep.

That's the tricky technical term for the way in which the desert wind smashes rocks into smithereens. Aeolian's ancient Greek for wind. Rather long-winded, if you ask me.

But the simple answer is that sand is made up of minuscule fragments of rock between 0.2 and 2 millimetres wide. Which is this big…

2 Sand isn't always, er, sandy coloured. Sometimes, it's black, or grey, or green. It all depends on the type of rock it's made from.

3 Some geographers have another theory for how some sandy deserts were made. According to them, the sand was spread by horrible hurricanes. It's difficult to say if they're right or wrong. After all, these hurricanes happened 18,000 years ago, and even your geography teacher can't remember that far back.

4 Strictly speaking, the superstar Sahara's the sandiest desert in the world. But that's only because it's so bloomin' big. Otherwise, the largest single stretch of sand is the Rub al Khali, or Empty Quarter, in the Arabian Desert. It covers an area of 560,000 square kilometres – about the same size as France. Fantastique. But don't expect to find shops selling ze fine French bread and cheese. It's not called empty for nothing.

5 Picture the scene. You're in the desperate desert, dreaming of slurping an ice-cold drink, when suddenly the sand bursts into song!

Yes, you heard right the first time – the sand starts singing. What does it sound like? It depends. Sometimes it's a deep, booming hum or a squeaky soprano. Geographers don't know for certain what sets the sand off. One theory is that it's because each sand grain has a coating of a shiny chemical called silica. This makes the sand grains stick together. When you step on a sand dune, you scatter the sand and the movement makes it sing. Or something. You could say it's a case of sand tunes, not sand dunes. Ahem.

Local people don't agree. "Singing?" they say. "Pah!" It's actually the sound of sinister sand-spirits laughing their socks off at stranded travellers. Or the sound of a bell coming from a monastery buried beneath the sand. Ding! Dong!

6 If you think that's weird, spare a thought for the people of Lyon, France. They woke up on 17 October 1846, to find that their city had gone ... rusty!

I'VE ONLY JUST HAD THIS PAINTED

What had happened was this. Far away, in the sand-strewn Sahara, tonnes of red sand had been picked up by wind. It later fell as blood-red rain. When the rain dried, it left behind what looked like a thinish coating of rust. No wonder they were worried.

7 Sometimes the wind whips up the sand into a frenzy. Woe betide you if you're caught in a sandstorm. It can sting your skin, make you choke and even strip the paint off a car. The best thing to do is to crouch down low and cover your face and eyes.

An especially savage sandstorm hit Egypt in March 1988. Howling winds hurled tonnes of sand into the air. In Cairo alone, six people died and 250 were injured. Many others had trouble breathing.

It's hard to imagine what being stuck in a sandstorm must be like. Here's how one eyewitness – an explorer called Richard Trench – described the experience:

Teacher teaser

Desperate to get out of double geography? Why not smile weakly at your teacher and say:

PLEASE, MISS, I'M NOT FEELING VERY WELL, THE SAND'S GIVEN ME A HEADACHE!

Is there a grain of truth in what you are saying?

Answer: Amazingly, there is. At least it worked for German geographer Herr van der Esch. Sandstorms made his head throb horribly. Why? Well, during a sandstorm billions and billions of grains of sand smash into each other. This creates friction* which sends static electricity crackling through the air. And this gives some people a splitting headache. Painful.

*Friction's a force that happens when two objects try to push past each other and slow each other down. Like when you're late for a lesson and you're running down the school corridor and you bash into someone coming the other way. Or when Camilla tries to push in at a waterhole. Ouch!

Sand-astic sand dunes

Did you know that there are seas in the desert? Sandy seas, of course. Complete with sandy waves. How can that be? Well, as the wind blows across the desert, it piles the sand up into giant wave-like dunes. The biggest sand dunes stand 200 metres high (that's 20 times taller than your house) and 900 metres wide.

Imagine building a sandcastle that big on the beach. Each dune contains billions and billions of sand grains and weighs millions and millions of tonnes.

One man with a really soft spot for sand dunes was British soldier and scientist, Brigadier Ralph Bagnold (1896-1990). When he wasn't off fighting, he was studying sand. His big break came in the 1930s when he was stationed in Egypt and Libya. There he led lots of expeditions into the Sahara Desert to study the effects of wind-blown sand. Yawn! Back home in England, he built himself a wind tunnel where he could carry on his sandy studies. What do you think he found out about sand?

THE WORLD'S FINEST HANDLEBAR MOUSTACHE

a) that sand is scattered about the desert willy nilly.

b) that the wind makes set patterns in the sand.

c) that camels kick the sand up into dunes.

Answer: b) Sand dunes don't just happen by accident. The wind blows the sand into different patterns which are repeated again and again. The size and shape of sand dunes depends on the speed and direction of the wind. Brainy Bagnold set out his ideas in a book called *The Physics of Blown Sand and Desert Dunes*. Which might sound deadly boring to you but it's riveting bedtime reading for budding geographers.

Spotter's guide to sand dunes
Having trouble sorting your seifs from your barchans? Getting your transverses in a twist? Don't worry. Help is at hand. Why not sneak a look at Brigadier Bagnold's very own notebook. You'll soon be able to make sense of sand. (Note: Of course, these aren't the Brigadier's actual notebooks. They're lost in the sands of time.)

47

1 Barchan – Crescent-shaped sand dunes. They form when the wind blows steadily from one direction. Here's one I made earlier in my wind tunnel:

a) The wind blows the sand along. If it meets an obstacle, like a boulder, a bush or a dead camel, the flow slows down.

b) The sand settles and starts to pile up.

c) It's blown up the side, higher and higher...

d) Until it reaches the top.

e) Then it topples and spills down the other side.

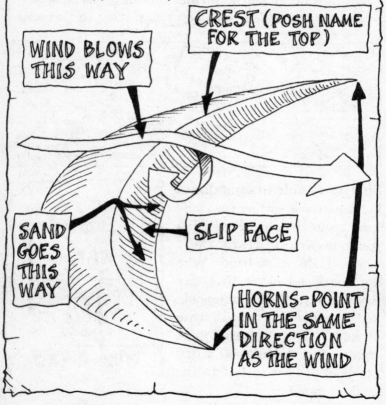

CREST (POSH NAME FOR THE TOP)

WIND BLOWS THIS WAY

SAND GOES THIS WAY

SLIP FACE

HORNS-POINT IN THE SAME DIRECTION AS THE WIND

2. Seif (sayf) — It's Arabic for sword. And sword's a very good name for these beauties because of their knife-sharp crests. They're snaky S-shaped dunes formed when the wind blows from two opposite directions. They're tall, growing up to 200 metres high, and up to 100 kilometres long.

WIND BLOWS THIS WAY

3 Transverse — Long, rounded ridges of sand, like giant sandy waves. Can be up to 300 kilometres long. They form at right angles to the wind. The valleys between them are so straight and true, you could drive a truck along them.

WIND BLOWS THIS WAY

4 Star – (My personal favourites, R.B.) They're formed when the wind keeps changing direction. And they look like giant starfish sneaking across the sand. Though if I saw a starfish this big in front of me, I'd be off like the wind...

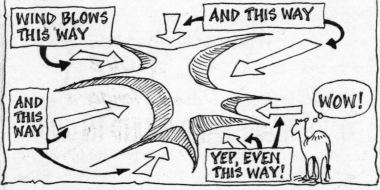

Earth-shattering fact

Sand dunes can move. It's true! As the wind blows sand over the top, the dune creeps forward. Very shifty. Woe betide anything that gets in its way. Whole towns and villages can be buried. And these dastardly dunes are horribly fickle. They drift along dustily for years and years, then suddenly change direction. There could be one heading your way. Time to get shovelling. And it means that the desert landscape is constantly changing, which can be very disorientating for travellers.

Secrets of the sand

Apart from towns and villages, many other deep secrets lie buried beneath the desert sand. Some have been there for years. Millions of years. Are you daring enough to go dinosaur hunting?

July 1923

The Daily Globe 🌍
The Gobi Desert, Mongolia

DINO GRAVEYARD FOUND IN GOBI

Ace American explorer, Roy Chapman Andrews, was today enjoying his new-found fame.

A team of experts led by Andrews has just unearthed a batch of fossilized dinosaur eggs – the first ever known. Andrews, who cuts a dashing figure in a wide-brimmed hat complete with feather, was understandably thrilled.

TICKLED PINK

"In spite of the pessimistic predictions before our start," he told our reporter, as he posed for a photograph, "we have opened a new world to science."

Dodging desert danger

He has every reason to be pleased. Very pleased. The 13 oblong-shaped eggs were found in one of the remotest parts of the Gobi Desert, a place as empty and unwelcoming as the surface of the moon. Andrews told us how the team had to travel

51

hundreds of kilometres through the desert to reach them, braving sandstorms and bandit attacks on the way. Instead of camels, the team travelled in a fleet of converted Dodge motor cars, another expedition first.

DUNE BUGGY

Ancient egg-snatcher caught

Experts have been given the chance to examine the extraordinary eggs and believe they may have been laid some 80 million years ago. They were perfectly preserved by the bone-dry heat and soft desert sand, remaining hidden and untouched ... until the American team found them.

SCRAMBLED EGGS

But that wasn't all Andrews discovered. More prehistoric surprises were to come. A further search revealed the bones of a small, toothless dinosaur near the nest, apparently caught red-handed as it tried to steal the eggs.

I'll be back, says Andrews

Before returning to his post at the American Museum of Natural History in New York, USA, Andrews plans to lead several more fossil-finding expeditions. "This is just the start," he said. "There may be hundreds more desert dinosaurs waiting to be discovered." And judging by what he's unearthed so far, things should get very exciting. Readers of the *Daily Globe* will be kept right up-to-date with the latest developments. With our exclusive coverage, it'll be just as if you were actually there.

RAIDERS OF THE LOST EGGS

Them dry bones

Dashing Roy C. Andrews turned out to be right. There were loads more desert dinosaurs. He went on to find more dinosaur eggs and other fantastic fossils. His desert digs turned him into a star. The museum promoted him to director (not bad for someone who started out sweeping the floor) and he had a dinosaur named in his honour – *Protoceratops andrewsi*. (Why not try naming a dinosaur after your teacher?) He also wrote several bestselling books, including the gripping *In the Last Days of the Dinosaurs*.

Since then, scientists from all over the world have tried their luck in the dinosaur graveyard. And they haven't been disappointed. So far, they've dug up the bones of hundreds of dinosaurs, not to mention mammals and reptiles. The most exciting find of all was a dinosaur with feathers. It proved what scientists had thought all along – that early birds were descended from dinosaurs.

Desperate desert fact file

NAME: Gobi Desert

LOCATION: Central Asia (China and Mongolia)

SIZE: 1,040,000 sq km

TEMPERATURE: Hot summers up to 45°C; bitterly cold winters down to −40°C

RAINFALL: 50–100 mm a year

DESERT TYPE: Inland

DESERT DATA:

- In Mongolian, its name means "waterless place".
- It's the coldest desert in the world (apart from Antarctica).
- Most of it isn't sandy but bare rock and stones, with massive mountains on three sides.
- It's home to Bactrian camels (they're the ones with two humps).

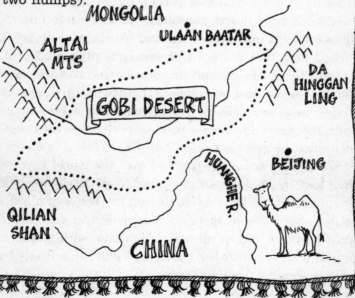

Designer deserts

Where do you find giant mushrooms and upside-down boats? And huge, stony tables? In the desperate desert, of course. They're all rocks carved into shapes by the weather.

HE TRIED TO PICK A MUSHROOM ROCK!

Over millions of years, the weather wears the desperate desert landscape away. Geographically speaking, this wearing away's called erosion. Time to check out the main earth-movers-and-shapers involved:

- Horrible heat and cold. Baking hot days and freezing cold nights have an earth-shattering effect on the desert. By day, the rocks get hot and expand. At night, they shrink in the cold. Then the whole thing starts all over again. Day after day. Eventually, all this heating and cooling takes its toll. There's an ear-piercing BAAANNGG! as the rocks split apart at the seams and shatter into pieces.

BANG!

- Rare rainfall. In the desert, it never rains but it pours. A sudden downpour can devastate the landscape. One minute it's dry as a bone, the next there's a flash flood racing towards you.

ONE MINUTE IT'S CHUCKING ROCKS AT ME, NOW IT'S TRYING TO DROWN ME!

(It's called a flash flood because it happens in a flash. Simple.) Flash floods carve out deep-sided gashes in the rocks, and sweep along tonnes of sand and boulders. When the rain stops, the water slows down and dumps its load. Then it evaporates. Just like that.

- Wild wind. Apart from stirring up sand dunes, the wind sends the grains of sand bouncing across the ground. Geographers call this saltation (which is Latin for leaping and jumping). Here's what happens:

1 The wind picks up a sand grain from the ground.

WIND

GRAIN OF SAND

2 It leaps up into the air.

MORE WIND

WHAT THE...

SAME GRAIN OF SAND

3 Then falls to the ground.

4 Then the whole thing starts again…

5 Sending the sand grain bouncing across the ground. Boingggg!

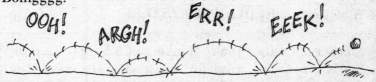

What on Earth has this got to do with erosion? Well, the wind blasts the sand at the desert rocks, wearing them away like a gigantic, and I mean gigantic, piece of sandpaper. But the sand can't bounce up very high. Instead it scrapes away at the rock close to the ground but can't reach up to the top. This goes on for years, until you're left with a rock shaped just like a mega-huge mushroom! Can you spot the difference?

Could you be a desert geomorphologist?

A geomorphologist (gee-ow-morf-ologist) is a horrible geographer who studies desert features. Well, it beats being called a boring old sand scientist. Fancy giving it a go when you leave school? (What d'you mean? You're not that desperate?) See if you've got what it takes with this quick-sand quiz.

1 An *erg* is a deadly desert disease. TRUE/FALSE
2 A *reg* is a one-humped camel. TRUE/FALSE
3 A *wadi* is a dried-up desert river. TRUE/FALSE
4 A *mesa* is a type of mountain. TRUE/FALSE
5 A *feche feche* is a fierce desert wind. TRUE/FALSE
6 A *playa* is a salty lake. TRUE/FALSE

Answers: 1 False. You're thinking of a l-erg-y. Geddit? *Erg* is the Arabic word for a vast sand sea covered in shifting sand dunes. Remember the lonely old Empty Quarter in the Arabian Desert? It's an enormous *erg*. **2** False. That's a dromedary – you're not even close! Though it's quite a cool name for a camel. *Reg* is the Arabic word for a stony, pebbly desert. It looks a bit like an old-fashioned cobbled street. **3** True. It's a deep gash or valley gouged out by a flash flood. A *wadi* can be dry for years and years, until a heavy downpour fills it with rain. Then you get a rare desert river.

"WADI'S" GOING ON HERE!

4 True. Geographically speaking, a *mesa* is a type of flat-topped mountain. It's left sticking up when the land all around it has been eroded away.

WE WANT A NICE, TIDY DESERT... SO CLEAN UP THIS "MESA"

It also happens to be the Spanish word for table. But never mind knives and forks or table cloths. Some *mesas* are so enormous, you could fit a whole village on the table top. **5 False.** *Feche feche* is actually very soft sand with a deceptively hard crust on top. It can measure just a few metres across or carry on for several kilometres. To be avoided at all costs, especially if you're in a car. Chances are it'll get you horribly bogged down. **6 True.** Usually a *playa*'s dry as a bone but it fills up with water after heavy rain. When the water dries up in the sun, it leaves a layer of sun-baked salt behind. *Playas* are the flattest places on Earth. Flat as pancakes. Which is great news for space shuttle pilots. How? Well, one large *playa* in California, USA, is used as a landing site for the space shuttle. Cosmic.

HEY! DID YOU "PLAYA" WITH THESE CONTROLS?

OK. You've been walking for days and days. You've seen enough sand dunes and mushroom rocks to last you a lifetime but you haven't yet met a living thing – plant, animal or human. And you're beginning to feel a bit lonely. Desperate for company? Great news! Find out who or what is waiting to meet you as you drift over the page...

A desert may look deathly quiet and deserted but in geography things aren't always what they seem. Despite the horribly hostile conditions, desperate deserts are surprisingly lively and lived in. For hundreds of hardy plants and animals, deserts are home, sweet, home. So why don't they get all hot and bothered? Prepare for a sizzling surprise or two.

Keeping cool

If you despair at the thought of double geography, try spending a day in a desert. Don't fancy it? Talk about sticking your head in the sand! Luckily, there are dozens of daring creatures who call the desert home. But how on Earth do they do it? How do they cope with the heat and the drought? There are two main secrets to staying alive.

a) Finding water. All living things need water to survive. (And that includes you.) Otherwise their body bits can't function properly.

b) Staying cool. It's hot in the desert. Dead hot. Especially during the day. (That's why you don't actually see many animals. They're all fast asleep somewhere nice and cool. Zzzzzz.)

OK, so neither of these things are a problem in your geography classroom, with its leaky roof and its heating which never works. But in the desert they're a matter of life and death. Try this cool quiz to find out how some desert creatures cope.

Chill out quiz

1 What does a darkling beetle drink?
a) Rain.
b) Fog.
c) Cactus juice.

2 How does a sandgrouse fetch water for its chicks?
a) In its beak.
b) In a bucket.
c) In its feathers.

3 What does a ground squirrel use as a sunshade?
a) Its tail.

b) Its mate.

c) A camel.

4 How does the desert tortoise cool down?
a) It stays inside its shell.
b) It pees on its back legs.
c) It rubs spit on its head.

5 What does a fennec fox use its ears for?
a) Radiators.
b) Fans.
c) Er … hearing.

6 How do spadefoot toads stand the heat?
a) By living underwater.
b) By living under a cactus.
c) By sleeping underground.

7 How often do kangaroo rats have a drink?
a) Never.
b) Twice a year.
c) Once a month.

8 How do snakes cross the hot sand without getting burnt?
a) By hitching a lift on a camel.

b) By flying over the sand.

c) By slithering sideways.

Answers:

1 b) This beetle lives in the bone-dry Namib where it doesn't rain for months on end. So what does it drink if there isn't any water? Well, this ingenious insect drinks fog that rolls in off the sea. On misty nights, it stands on its head on a seaside sand dune, wiggling its back legs in the air. The fog condenses on to its body, then trickles down into its mouth. Brilliant, eh?

2 c) The sandgrouse lays its eggs in the scorching Saharan sand. The trouble is there's nothing for its thirsty chicks to drink. So the male sandgrouse flies off to an oasis and dives into the water. His feathers are specially designed to soak up water like a sponge. Back home, the chicks simply suck his feathers to get at the water. Simple. The sandgrouse is a doting dad – fetching the water often means a round trip of 100 kilometres or more.

3 a) The Kalahari ground squirrel uses its big, bushy tail as a parasol. It holds it over its baking body, at a jaunty angle, to give as much shade as it can.

4 b) When it gets really hot, the desert tortoise pees all over its back legs. Embarrassing but true! The pee dries in the sun and cools the toasted tortoise down.

5 a) The fennec fox uses its enormous ears to give off warmth, a bit like huge, furry radiators. Blood vessels flow across the surface of each ear, carrying warm blood with them. As air blows across them, it cools the blood (and the fox) down. Of course, the fox's ears also make brilliant, er, fox's ears, for listening out for juicy gerbils. Yum, yum!

6 c) Spadefoot toads spend nine months asleep in cool, underground burrows, lined with nice, damp slime. But at the first sign of rain, they leap into action. They hot-foot it to the nearest pool and lay their eggs in the water. Within two weeks, the eggs have hatched into tadpoles, the tadpoles have turned into frogs, and the frogs have hopped off into the desert. Then it's bedtime again.

7 a) Believe it or not, kangaroo rats never have a drink. They get all the water they need from seeds. Thirsty hawks and coyotes don't need to drink either. They simply gobble up a thirst-quenching kangaroo rat.

8 c) During the day, the acrobatic sidewinder rattlesnake has a clever way of getting across hot sand. It flips its body sideways and launches itself across the sand. In this way, its body only touches the sand for a few seconds and doesn't get burnt. Normally, though, sidewinders try to avoid the daytime heat and only get out and about at night when it's cool.

Snake, rattle and roll

Many desert snakes are poisonous. Deadly poisonous. To make matters worse, they're almost exactly the same colour as sand which makes them horribly hard to spot. Rattlesnakes have particularly poisonous reputations. But are they really as sinister as they seem? Some years ago we sent our *Daily Globe* reporter to find out more about them. And who better to ask than the world's leading expert on rattlesnakes, Laurence M. Klauber (1883–1968), also known as Mr Rattlesnake. He spent 35 years studying, dissecting and writing about rattlesnakes. If he didn't know the answers no one would. Here's what he had to say.

When did you start getting interested in rattlesnakes?

When I was a boy in California. We didn't live too far from the desert, you see, where plenty of rattlesnakes live. I was really hooked on reptiles. But I was 40 years old before I started studying them seriously.

What did you do before that then?

I worked for an electrical company. I started off selling electric signs and ended up as president. I was really very lucky. But my real love was always reptiles.

So why did you leave?

I wanted to spend more time with the reptiles. So I became Curator of Reptiles at San Diego Zoo. They'd got several snakes they couldn't identify and they called me in to help. And I never left. It was a dream come true!

Do you ever take your work home?

Sure I do. I've got 35,000 rattlesnakes and assorted reptiles pickled in jars in my basement.

Gulp! And where did you get all those snakes from?

From the desert, mainly. If you're interested, a spring night's the ideal time to go. That's when the rattlesnakes are most active. Sacks are the best thing for catching them in.

Er, no, thanks, I'll give it a miss. And are rattlesnakes really deadly?

Not if you treat them nicely they're not. They'll only turn nasty if you get on their nerves. If you don't disturb them, they won't attack you. But if one starts rattling, turn around calmly and start to walk away. Whatever you do, keep your distance.

I'll take your word for it. Have you ever been bitten?

Er, yes, but only once or twice. I was lucky, it wasn't a particularly poisonous snake. The most dangerous rattlesnake is the eastern diamondback. Its markings make it tricky to spot and its bite can be fatal to humans.

Right. And what's all this about a rattle?

RATTLE!

The rattle's made up of hollow, scaly rings at the tip of the rattlesnake's tail. When the snake shakes it, it makes a buzzing sound. Sounds quite eerie, in fact. It's meant to warn enemies to leave well alone. If they don't, the snake will strike. Also, you can tell individual rattlesnakes apart by the number of rings in their rattles.

Any tips for not getting rattled?

WHERE'D SHE GO?

Yes. Wear a good pair of boots and a long pair of thick trousers, that's my advice. Then you might stand a chance. And if you're bitten, get yourself along to a doctor fast. Oh dear, are you feeling all right?

Earth-shattering fact

Forget rattlesnake-proof trousers. The deadliest creature in the desperate desert is the desert locust. Alone, these little fellows look small and harmless (one could perch happily on your thumb). But they never travel alone. These unstoppable insects fly around in swarms up to ONE THOUSAND MILLION strong. And they're horribly hungry! They devastate farmers' fields, devouring every plant in sight. What a swarm can guzzle in ONE DAY would feed 500 people for a year. Farmers have tried spraying them with super-strong insecticides but nothing seems to spoil their awesome appetites.

Design a desert-creature competition

Think you could do better? Why not enter our hot new competition to design the perfect desert animal? The fabulous first prize is an unforgettable camel safari through the record-breaking Sahara Desert. (Can I come with you?) Don't forget, you need to come up with a creature that can cope with baking heat, freezing cold, sandstorms, dust and lack of water. So it needs to be pretty special. Any ideas yet? Here's a clue – there's one desert animal that would win first prize in any creature feature competition (as long as it wasn't a beauty contest). Its survival skills are second to none. Can you guess what it is? Give in? It's the amazingly adaptable ... camel, of course. Forget cats and dogs. Camels are my favourite animals. And here's my very own Camilla to model the latest in camel cool ...

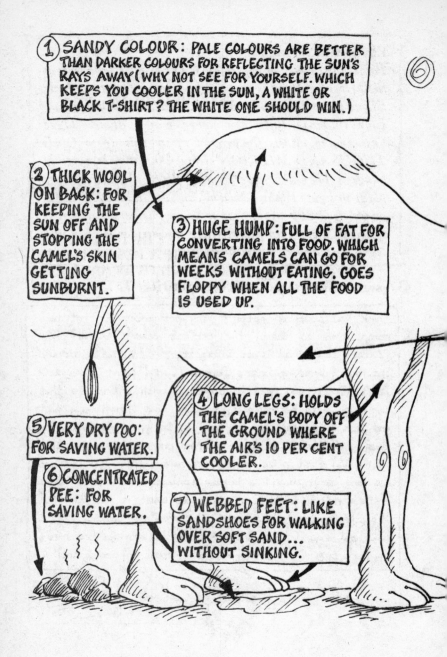

1 SANDY COLOUR: PALE COLOURS ARE BETTER THAN DARKER COLOURS FOR REFLECTING THE SUN'S RAYS AWAY (WHY NOT SEE FOR YOURSELF. WHICH KEEPS YOU COOLER IN THE SUN, A WHITE OR BLACK T-SHIRT? THE WHITE ONE SHOULD WIN.)

2 THICK WOOL ON BACK: FOR KEEPING THE SUN OFF AND STOPPING THE CAMEL'S SKIN GETTING SUNBURNT.

3 HUGE HUMP: FULL OF FAT FOR CONVERTING INTO FOOD. WHICH MEANS CAMELS CAN GO FOR WEEKS WITHOUT EATING. GOES FLOPPY WHEN ALL THE FOOD IS USED UP.

5 VERY DRY POO: FOR SAVING WATER.

6 CONCENTRATED PEE: FOR SAVING WATER.

4 LONG LEGS: HOLDS THE CAMEL'S BODY OFF THE GROUND WHERE THE AIR'S 10 PER CENT COOLER.

7 WEBBED FEET: LIKE SANDSHOES FOR WALKING OVER SOFT SAND... WITHOUT SINKING.

AND I'M GORGEOUS TOO!

⑧ TWO PAIRS OF EXTRA-LONG EYELASHES: FOR KEEPING OUT THE SAND.

⑨ STRETCHY NOSTRILS: CAN BE CLOSED IN A SANDSTORM TO KEEP SAND OUT.

⑩ TOUGH TEETH: FOR CHEWING THE THORNIEST DESERT PLANTS WHICH NO OTHER ANIMAL WILL TOUCH. (AND TENTS)

⑪ THIN HAIR ON TUM: LETS HEAT ESCAPE FROM THE CAMEL'S BODY TO COOL THE CAMEL DOWN.

Some hump-backed facts about camels

1 Can't tell one camel from another? Simple – just count their humps. A one-humped camel is called a dromedary. It lives in Arabia, Asia and Africa. Two-humped camels are Bactrians. They come from the Gobi. They get through the freezing winter by growing a shaggy, woolly coat.

I'M GLAD I REMEMBERED TO PUT MY COAT ON!

2 Camels can go for days and days without a drop to drink. But they work up a terrible thirst. And when they do get to water, they can guzzle down an awesome 130 litres in just 15 MINUTES! That would be like you drinking 400 cans of pop. You'd definitely go pop after that lot.

3 You wouldn't have recognized the first ever camels. They had short, stumpy legs and were the size of pigs. And they didn't have humps. They lived about 40 million years ago in North America (but you don't get camels there any more).

4 Camels are horribly useful. For a start, they can walk for miles without food or water. And carry loads of up to 100 kilograms (that's like you and two of your friends). Very handy for humping your tent about. And unlike cars and other desert vehicles, camels don't get bogged down in the sand.

5 Some desert people rely on camels for their living. They buy and sell them at camel markets (the white ones are worth the most). The more camels you have, the better off you are. Fewer than 20 is nothing to boast about. But 50 or more means you're rich. Camels also make brilliant wedding presents.

IT'S NOT ANOTHER TOASTER, IS IT?

6 And that's not all. People make tents and carpets from camel hair, and bags and rope from their hide. They even use camel pee to wash their hair. Apparently it leaves your hair nice and shiny and kills any irritating lice. Are you brave enough to give it a go?

7 Camel milk is crammed full of goodness and is rich in vital Vitamin C. (It's good for your teeth and bones. If you don't fancy a nice hot cup of camel milk before bedtime, you can also find it in fruit and veg.) You can either drink it straight, let it go off a bit or make it into yummy yoghurt. It tastes a bit like runny fudge. Fancy a spoonful?

FUDGE-FLAVOURED CAMEL YOGHURT RECIPE

Ingredients:
• some camel milk

Equipment:
• a large pan
• a bag made out of a goatskin
• a tripod made out of three sticks
• some rope

What you do:

1 Milk your camel. (Mind it doesn't kick you.)

2 Put the camel milk in the pan and heat it over the fire.

3 When it's warm but not boiling, pour it into the goatskin bag.

4 Hang the bag from the tripod, using the rope.

5 Give the bag a good shake. Repeat every few minutes for about two and a half hours until the mixture's thickened up a bit. (Warning: it will make your arm ache.)
6 Now tip it into bowls and serve it up to your friends. (If you dare …)

Horrible Health Warning

Camels aren't called "ships of the desert" for nothing. After an hour or two of sitting on a camel's back and swaying to and fro, you'll be feeling horribly seasick.

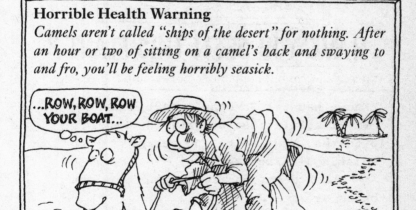

Desert plant dilemmas

Life's no picnic either for desert plants. Like animals, they need water to live. Without it, they'd shrivel up and die. In fact, they need water to make their food. Pretty vital, eh? Yet an amazing number of plucky plants live in the bone-dry desert. So how on Earth do they do it? It's a bloomin' miracle. Take the most famous desert plant of all, the skyscraping saguaro cactus...

WANTED

HAVE YOU SEEN THIS PLANT?

Name: SAGUARO CACTUS

Known haunts: Sonoran Desert, USA

Vital statistics: Height: 18 m. Weight: 10 tonnes. Age: up to 200 years.

Distinguishing features:

• Thick stem: for storing up to eight tonnes of water.

• Groovy pleats: lets stem double in size to fit all that water in.

• Waxy skin: to seal moisture in.

• Sharp spines: large leaves leak loads of water into the air. Fine spines lose much less. They also shade the cacti from the sun. And see off creatures who fancy a nibble.

- Roots: shallow and branching for sucking up as much rain as possible as soon as it hits the ground.
- Elf owl: nests in a hole inside the cactus. If it's an elf owl, it must be a saguaro. (Though it's not strictly a distinguishing feature.)

Any known accomplices: About 2,000 suspects, including the barrel cactus, teddy bear cactus, beavertail cactus, old man cactus, hedgehog cactus, organ pipe cactus, to name a few.

Any known enemies: Ruthless cacti rustlers who go around stealing cacti from the desert without getting a permit. They cart them off and sell them to budding gardeners. Stolen saguaros can fetch around US $1,200 (£750) for a cactus 5 metres tall, with an extra $50 (£30) bonus for each extra arm. In Arizona, there's now a full-time cactus cop to round up the rustlers.

Warning! This plant is armed and dangerous. A very prickly character indeed. Do not go near it. Even if you're dying for a drink. Especially if you're dying for a drink. Its juice is horribly poisonous to humans.

If you spot a cactus in the Sahara, something's gone horribly wrong. Cacti only grow in the USA. So it's either a mirage (see page 104) or you're in the wrong desert. Oops!

OOPS! I'M IN THE WRONG DESERT

Desperate desert fact file

NAME: Sonoran Desert

LOCATION: South-west USA and Mexico

SIZE: 310,000 sq km

TEMPERATURE: Hot summers from 41°C; cold winters to 3°C and below

RAINFALL: 50–250 mm a year

DESERT TYPE: High pressure

DESERT DATA:

● It's home to masses of wildlife, including pronghorn antelopes and mountain lions.

● It's prone to earthquakes because it lies close to the shaky San Andreas Fault, a colossal crack in the Earth.

● It's one of several North American deserts. You'll also find the Great Basin Desert, the Mojave Desert, the Painted Desert and the Chihuahuan Desert (yep, like those diddy dogs).

Bloomin' marvellous

Now, cacti may be the most famous plants in the desert but they're not the only ones. I've come across some marvellous bloomers on my travels. Here are some other ways in which these parched plants track down life-saving water. Ingenious, I think you'll agree.

One of the most down-to-earth desert plants is the marvellous mesquite bush. With roots an amazing 20 metres long, it can really get to the root of the problem. And the problem is finding water. Its roots reach down deep under the desert to suck up underground water. It's a bit like you slurping a drink through a 20-metre-long straw.

The cunning creosote bush does the opposite. Its tiny roots branch out far and wide to suck up dew and rain from all over the surface. Clever, eh?

MMM, TASTY TOO

CREOSOTE BUSH

MESQUITE BUSH

The weird welwitschia of the Namib looks just like a giant turnip. At least, that's what it looked like to me. Except for the long, leathery leaves sticking out of the top. This peculiar plant only has two leaves but they can grow up to 3 metres long. They trail over the ground, getting terribly ragged and tattered at the edges. But they're also horribly helpful. They soak up fog blowing in off the sea and keep the wind-blown welwitschia well watered.

OOOH, BREAKFAST

Last but not least, my own personal favourite. For most of the time, as you know, deserts look desperately dry and deserted. But in summer, when there's the best chance of some rain, it's a different story. Then the desert bursts into bloom. How? Well, there are billions of seeds buried under the ground. They've been there since the last time it rained, months or even years ago. As soon as it rains, the seeds start to sprout. And in no time at all, the desert's decked out in fields of brilliantly coloured wildflowers, like desert daisies and dandelions. Now that's what I call bloomin' lovely.

But how on Earth do these flowers pick the best time to bloom? The truth is that these secretive seeds have a very special coating. It contains a chemical which stops the seeds sprouting until there's plenty of rain. Enough, in fact, to soak into the ground and wash the coating off. It's just as well. If the seeds tried to grow during a light shower, they'd soon wither and die when the sun came out again.

And finally...

Speaking of secretive, spare a thought for the desperate devil's hole pupfish. Its only home is a tiny underground pool in the middle of the desert. The rest of its habitat has all dried up. So the poor old pupfish has NOWHERE ELSE TO GO. Put yourself in the penned-in pupfish's place. Imagine being stuck in your geography classroom for ever. Now that's a horrible thought.

Desert living may be cool for camels. But what about human beings? Surely the desert's too hot for them to handle? Well, incredibly it isn't. Despite the desperately harsh conditions, a mind-boggling 650 million people, that's 13 per cent of the world's population, live in the deadly deserts. And they've been doing it for years and years. They've found ways of coping with the heat and finding water that would put you to shame. But don't be fooled into thinking it's easy for them. Life in the desert can be horribly hard. Are you ready to find out how they do it? Why not spend a day with Sandy and the San people of the Kalahari Desert in Africa…

MY NOTEBOOK
A DAY IN THE LIFE OF THE SAN
by Sandy

Hi, Sandy here. I'm here in the Kalahari, spending the day with the San people. It's such an honour to be here, I can't tell you. These are people who really know how to survive in the desert. They'll certainly be able to teach me a thing or two.

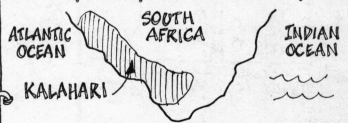

Dawn
It's dawn and time to get up and make a fire. It's pretty chilly in the desert first thing in the morning. Lucky I brought a blanket. There aren't any bathrooms in the desert, of course,

but a bush makes a good toilet. There's no water either, at least not to waste, so instead of a wash, the San rub red sand over their bodies. Actually, it works quite well. Breakfast is a couple of spoonfuls of porridge.

dirty

clean

NOTES:
To make a fire the traditional San way, you need to use a fire drill. No, not the sort where you hear a loud bell and file out into the playground. It's made of two long sticks. One stick has a hole in it which the other stick slots into. Then you twist the long stick around in your hands until you get a spark. Simple when you've had plenty of practice!

twist the stick backwards and forwards... very fast!

Early morning
After breakfast, the men set off hunting. They travel very light. All each hunter carries is a bag with his hunting spear, bow and arrows, digging stick (for finding water) and a fire drill (see Notes). I'm afraid I can't go with them this time but one of the

hunters told me what happens. After walking for miles and miles through the desert, they finally track down an antelope. (There's some extraordinary wildlife in the Kalahari. Not just antelopes, but elephants and giraffes, too. It's finding them that's the tricky bit. Luckily, the San hunters know the desert like the back of their hands.)

bow
arrows
animal skin bag

When they track the antelope down, they fire. Their arrows are tipped with poison squeezed from a small but deadly beetle. The antelope doesn't stand a chance.

Back at the camp...
While the men are away, I'm off into the desert with the women and children to search for seeds and roots to eat. These are an important part of the San's daily diet. But it's hard work finding enough of them. I spend most of the time swigging water from my water bottle. The San women laugh at me. They don't need water bottles. When they're thirsty, they look for a small, dried-up plant sticking out of the sand. Goodness knows how they spot it. Looks just like a twig to me. Then it's time to start digging. It turns out that the twig thing actually belongs to a large, round tuber (a swollen plant stem). If you squeeze it, it drips with water. Very clever.

tuber

Any spare water is stored in empty ostrich egg shells which are sealed up and buried for later.

NOTES:
The San are experts at finding water. Here's how they make a traditional "sipwell":

1 They find a patch of damp ground and dig a deep hole.

2 Then they stick a hollow reed into the hole, like a drinking straw.

3 They fill the hole up, with the reed straw sticking out.

4 Gradually, water collects round the end of the straw.

5 When someone's thirsty, they simply slurp it up.

reed straw

SUCK UP water

Later that day
We get back to the camp just before the men. They arrive carrying the antelope. They have a really ingenious way of cooking it. First the men skin the antelope, then bury it in a hole in the hot sand. Then they light a fire in the hole and cover the whole thing with sand. When the meat's cooked, they cut it into strips. Brilliant. Then it's time for a feast! Everyone's hungry. Nothing goes to waste. Some of the meat is eaten straightaway. (And it's delicious, I must say.) Some is saved and dried for

winter. The antelope's skin is made into bags and clothes, and its bones are used for arrows. The San even eat the gristly bits in its ears. After all, it may be a while before they catch another one.

Sunset

After the feast, when we're all feeling full, the San sing songs and dance around the campfire until late into the night. They tell me that it's to thank the spirits for giving them a good day's hunting. Dances are also believed to help heal sick people. The San sing songs which remember their ancestors and ask the spirits for rain. It's a peaceful end to a long and tiring day. Now I'm really ready for my bed. I could sleep anywhere but I'm given a space on the ground behind a simple wall woven from dried grass. Each of the San has their own space. It's dry and out of the wind. Goodnight.

Next day
Up at dawn. It's time for the San to pack up their few belongings and set off for another campsite. They can't stay in one place for more than a few days. There's simply not enough food or water. And it's time for me to say goodbye.

I've had a brilliant time with the San. They're very kind and hospitable people, even though their lives are horribly hard. After even one day, I don't know how they keep going. I'll never complain about anything again.

NOTES:
The San have lived in the desert for 30,000 years. But now their lives are changing. Many have been badly treated and are being forced to leave their land. They're being made to settle down in shanty towns instead. It's a dreadful thing to happen to them. Some San are desperately fighting back to save their homes and their ancient culture. Otherwise they and their traditional desert skills may die out for ever. And that would be a terrible tragedy.

Teacher teaser

If you want to see your teacher really lost for words, forget
Latin or ancient Greek. To confuse them utterly, speak
Click. Start off with the word, "//kx'a". Helpful hint: to
speak Click, it helps if you're good at pulling faces. Ready?
First, pull your tongue quickly away from the sides of your
mouth as if you're calling a horse. Then make a noise half-
way between 'k' and 'g'. Now make a little strangled sound as
if you're choking. (Don't really choke.) Then finish off with
an 'aaahhh'. Got all that? If you don't mind scaring yourself
to death, try practising in a mirror.

But what are you trying to say?

Answer: Click is the language spoken by the San. In Click,
"//kx'a" is the word for a type of tree. Click is horribly
difficult to speak or understand, and can take years and
years to master properly. And watch out. Even the tiniest
little mistake can change a word's meaning utterly.

Desperate desert fact file

NAME: Kalahari Desert
LOCATION: Southern Africa
SIZE: 520,000,000 sq km
TEMPERATURE: Hot summers up to 49°C; cool winters with temperatures below freezing
RAINFALL: 130–460 mm
DESERT TYPE: High pressure and inland
DESERT DATA:

• It's mostly covered by ancient sand seas and dunes which formed over 10,000 years ago.

• It's home to the bizarre baobab tree which stores water in its trunk. When it's full it can measure 30 metres around its middle.

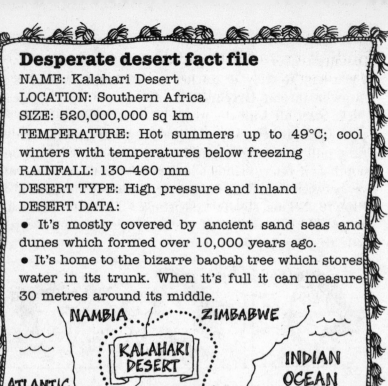

• It's also home to the ostrich, the world's largest bird – which lays the biggest birds' eggs. Eggs-cellent for storing water in.

EGGSCELLENT FOR STORING WATER

Finding a roof for the night

Many desert people are nomads. This means that they're constantly moving from place to place in search of food and water. They don't stay anywhere for long, just until supplies run out. Moving home all the time can get very tiring. In the desert, you can't just move from one ready-built house to another. There simply aren't any around. You have to carry your own home with you. So you need something that's quick to put up and take down, and that can be easily plonked on the back of your camel. Any ideas? What about a take-away desert tent?

Camping supplies catalogue

In a dilemma about which tent to choose? Don't worry. Our tents are specially designed to take the strain. Developed with the help of local desert people worldwide, they're ideal for camping out on the sand. We're proud to present our latest top-selling tent range...

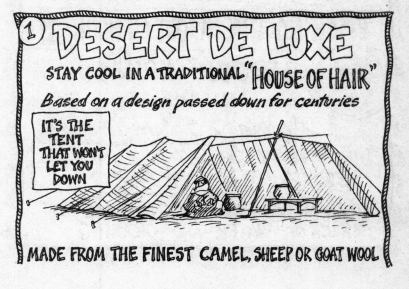

① DESERT DE LUXE

STAY COOL IN A TRADITIONAL "HOUSE OF HAIR"

Based on a design passed down for centuries

IT'S THE TENT THAT WON'T LET YOU DOWN

MADE FROM THE FINEST CAMEL, SHEEP OR GOAT WOOL

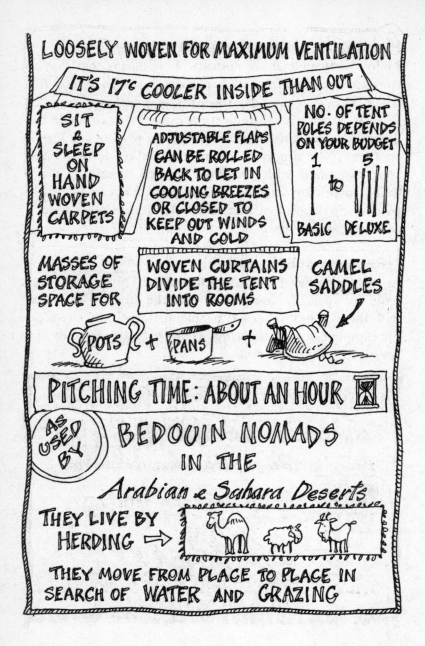

LOOSELY WOVEN FOR MAXIMUM VENTILATION

IT'S 17°C COOLER INSIDE THAN OUT

SIT & SLEEP ON HAND WOVEN CARPETS

ADJUSTABLE FLAPS CAN BE ROLLED BACK TO LET IN COOLING BREEZES OR CLOSED TO KEEP OUT WINDS AND COLD

NO. OF TENT POLES DEPENDS ON YOUR BUDGET
1 to 5
BASIC   DELUXE

MASSES OF STORAGE SPACE FOR

WOVEN CURTAINS DIVIDE THE TENT INTO ROOMS

CAMEL SADDLES

POTS + PANS +

PITCHING TIME: ABOUT AN HOUR

AS USED BY

BEDOUIN NOMADS IN THE
Arabian & Sahara Deserts

THEY LIVE BY HERDING ⇒

THEY MOVE FROM PLACE TO PLACE IN SEARCH OF WATER AND GRAZING

Snug as a bug

For those chilly desert nights. Choose a tent that really keeps out the cold...

"MONGOLIAN GER"

HOLE IN ROOF TO LET SMOKE OUT

FOLD-UP WOODEN FRAME FOR EASY TRANSPORTATION

COMPLETE WITH ITS OWN COOKING FIRE

MADE FROM WARM SHEEP'S WOOL AND FELT

LIGHTWEIGHT AND EASY TO DISMANTLE

STAY WARM IN WINTER AND COOL IN SUMMER

PITCHING TIME : 30 MINUTES

AS USED BY **MONGOL** NOMADS IN THE *GOBI DESERT*

THEY HERD SHEEP AND GOATS, MOVING ABOUT TEN TIMES A YEAR

Two-Season Tents

TWO TRADITIONAL TENTS TO CHOOSE FROM. MADE FROM LOCALLY AVAILABLE MATERIALS. BOTH EASILY PACKED UP AND PORTABLE

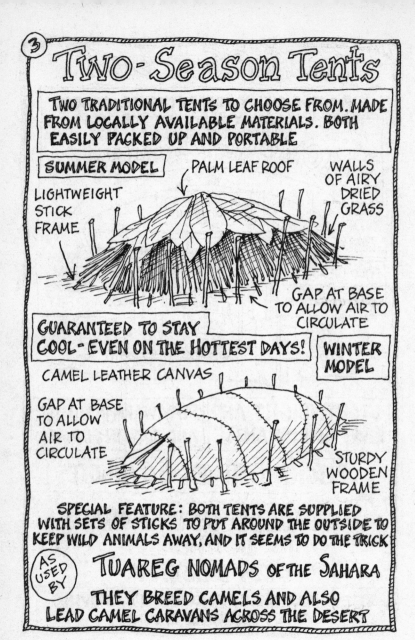

SUMMER MODEL

PALM LEAF ROOF

WALLS OF AIRY DRIED GRASS

LIGHTWEIGHT STICK FRAME

GAP AT BASE TO ALLOW AIR TO CIRCULATE

GUARANTEED TO STAY COOL - EVEN ON THE HOTTEST DAYS!

WINTER MODEL

CAMEL LEATHER CANVAS

GAP AT BASE TO ALLOW AIR TO CIRCULATE

STURDY WOODEN FRAME

SPECIAL FEATURE: BOTH TENTS ARE SUPPLIED WITH SETS OF STICKS TO PUT AROUND THE OUTSIDE TO KEEP WILD ANIMALS AWAY, AND IT SEEMS TO DO THE TRICK

AS USED BY

TUAREG NOMADS OF THE SAHARA

THEY BREED CAMELS AND ALSO LEAD CAMEL CARAVANS ACROSS THE DESERT

THE QUICK-FIX SHELTER

IF YOU ONLY NEED OVERNIGHT ACCOMMODATION

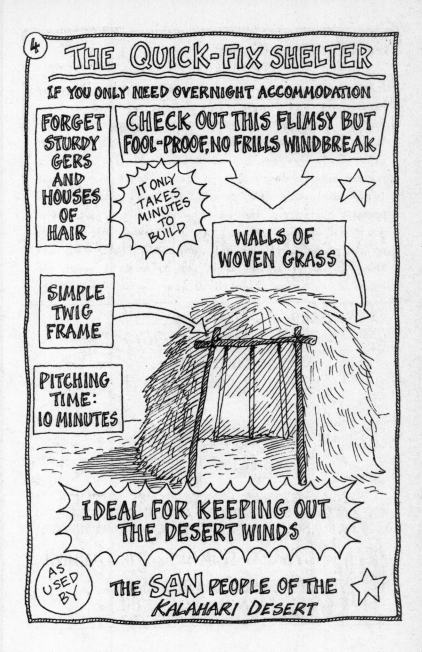

FORGET STURDY GERS AND HOUSES OF HAIR

CHECK OUT THIS FLIMSY BUT FOOL-PROOF, NO FRILLS WINDBREAK

IT ONLY TAKES MINUTES TO BUILD

WALLS OF WOVEN GRASS

SIMPLE TWIG FRAME

PITCHING TIME: 10 MINUTES

IDEAL FOR KEEPING OUT THE DESERT WINDS

AS USED BY

THE SAN PEOPLE OF THE KALAHARI DESERT

95

Dressed for the desert

Sandy here again, with a word of warning. If you're heading off into the desperate desert, you need to dress for the part. So what's the latest in desert fashion? Well, for a start, practicality's more important than style. So shorts and a T-shirt won't do, I'm afraid, no matter how good you look in them. Forget looking cool. It's keeping cool that counts. You need clothes that'll protect you from the sand, wind and sun. Otherwise you'll end up burnt to a crisp and looking like a dried-up old prune. (And just how un-cool is that!) The best thing to do, I always think, is to look at what the locals are wearing. Then model your clothes on theirs:

The Tuareg certainly know how to dress. And how to stay cool as a cucumber. So what's the secret of their success?

VERY NICE

MODEL NO 1: TUAREG NOMAD
OUTFIT: TRADITIONAL DRESS
SCORE: 10/10 (AN OLD DESERT HAND)

TURBAN: WOUND AROUND HIS HEAD AND NECK TO STOP SUNBURN

LOOSE-FLOWING ROBES: NOT ONLY PROTECT HIM FROM THE SUN BUT ALLOW COOL AIR TO CIRCULATE INSIDE

BLUE VEIL: COVERS HIS FACE AND MOUTH TO KEEP OUT SAND, DUST AND EVIL SPIRITS. TUAREG VEILS ARE DYED DEEP BLUE. (AND ONLY MEN WEAR THEM.)

LONG COTTON ROBES: TO PROTECT HIS WHOLE BODY

LEATHER SANDALS: FOR WALKING ACROSS HOT SAND

I've modelled my outfit on the Tuareg's. After all, it works for them. Personally, I think it looks really cool.

MODEL NO 2: SANDY
OUTFIT: TRENDY EXPLORER
SCORE: 8/10 (NOT BAD, THOUGH I SAY IT MYSELF!)

SUN HAT: ESSENTIAL, WIDE-BRIMMED IS BEST

SUNGLASSES: TO PROTECT YOUR EYES FROM THE GLARE

SCARF: FOR COVERING YOUR MOUTH AND NECK

BLANKET OR JUMPER: FOR THOSE COLD DESERT NIGHTS

STURDY BOOTS: MIND YOUR FEET DON'T GET BURNT

SHOW OFF!

LOOSE, LONG-SLEEVED SHIRT AND LONG BAGGY TROUSERS: FOR COOLNESS, COTTON'S BEST

Here's an example of how not to dress for exploring the desperate desert. Don't geography teachers know anything?

MODEL NO 3: MR TOMPKINSON
OUTFIT: GEOGRAPHY TEACHER
SCORE: 3/10 (DESPERATE! A REAL
FASHION VICTIM.)

THINNING HAIR: WHERE'S THAT HAT?

SHIRT AND TIE: FOR GETTING HOT UNDER THE COLLAR

TWEED JACKET: A BIT WORN AT THE ELBOWS

BROWN, SUEDE SHOES: THAT HOLE WILL SOON BE LETTING IN SAND

Tea-time desert style

Now that you've got the clothes, it's time to meet the locals. Generally speaking, desert people are very hospitable. Even if they've never met you before, they'll offer you food and a place to stay. (Of course, once they get to know you better, it might be a different story!) So, it's important not to upset or offend them. (In the desert, you need all the friends you can get.) Here's a quick, step-by-step guide to minding your manners if a Tuareg invites you in for a cup of tea.

Are you brave enough to take tea with a Tuareg?

1 You arrive in a Tuareg camp. Act casual but be polite. Say "How do you do?" and shake hands with everyone, as if you've got all the time in the world. The Tuareg don't like to be hurried.

2 You're offered a glass of sweet mint tea. Drink it quickly and make lots of slurping noises. (This shows you're enjoying it.)

3 You're offered another glass of tea, then another. (By the way, it's very rude to refuse.) If it stops at three, congratulations. It means you're welcome to stay.

4 If you're given another glass (your fourth), you're welcome but not that welcome. Time to be on your way. Drink your tea, then get up, say your goodbyes (slowly, mind), and go.

Settling down

Not all desert people are nomads like the Tuareg. I mean, would you fancy moving house all the time? If you like the desert so much you can't bear to leave, why not pick a nice shady spot and settle down? You'll need water, of course, for drinking and growing your crops. But this is the desert so where can you find it? Well, the surface of the desert may look dusty and dry but there are buckets (and I mean buckets) of water under the sun-baked ground. You just need to know where to look for it.

Getting it out can be tricky, though. You could dig a well (you'll need to dig deep). Or you could sit and wait for the water to seep to the surface of its own accord and create a fabulously fertile … oasis. (You might be waiting for a very long time – it could take 10,000 years for the water to surface.) Here's the inside story of how a flourishing oasis is formed.

1 Rain falls on the ground (it may be miles away) and soaks into tiny holes in the rock. This is called an aquifer. It's like a giant, rocky sponge. (Not great for using in the bath.)

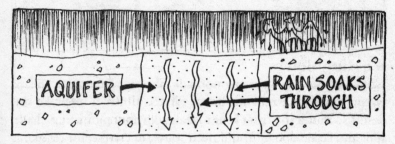

2 The water seeps along happily underground…

3 …until it comes to a split in the rocks and can't go any further. Then it's forced to the surface.

4 Welcome to an oasis!

How green-fingered are you? With all that water lying around, you can grow loads of lovely fruit and veg. Like apricots, wheat and grapes, for a start. And palm trees... You might not think it to look at them but palm trees are horribly hardy and useful. You can eat their fruit (dates) raw, cooked or dried (like the ones you get at Christmas). You can use their trunks for building, their leaves for baskets and their seeds for camel food. And how about a tasty palm-bud salad? Delicious!

Horrible Health Warning

But before you get too comfy and settled, remember that the desert can play tricks on your eyes. Tricks that can drive you mad with thirst. Picture the scene. You've run out of water and you're desperate for a drink. Just then, you spot an oasis ahead of you. Phew! You're saved. You think. But however fast you walk towards it, it just gets further and further away. That's because the oasis doesn't really exist. It isn't actually there. It's a mirage. And it's maddening.

What happens is this:

1 A layer of warm air lies next to the ground.
2 It's trapped by a layer of cool air above it.
3 The layers bend the light coming from the sky.
4 So you think you see a refreshing pool of water rippling on the horizon. Lovely! But it's actually a reflection of the sky. (Worse still, it looks like it's fringed with shady palm trees. Sorry, more tricks of the light.)

Can you spot the difference?

Desperate desert survival quiz

Congratulations! You've come this far and you're still alive. You're really getting the hang of this desert living lark. But what about your geography teacher? If he was stranded in the deserted desert, would he be able to survive? Or would his sense of adventure completely desert him? Try this deadly quiz on him to find out. All the answers are based on what local desert people would do in these situations. And they should know. After all, they've been surviving in the deadly desert since before your teacher was even born. And that's a very long time indeed!

1 You're in the Australian Desert and you're thirsty. Trouble is, there's no water for miles around. Just then, you hear a frog croaking. The sound seems to be coming from under the ground.

Do you bother to go and look for the frog? Yes/No

2 A diabolical dust storm is brewing in the Sahara Desert. You haven't got time to run for shelter so you decide to stand your ground and brave it out until the storm blows over.

Are you doing the right thing? Yes/No

3 You're in the Kalahari Desert with a group of San hunters. You're tracking an antelope when you spot a lion lurking in the bushes near by. You don't want to shout out a warning or the lion might hear you and charge.

San hunters have a range of hand signals to use in just this situation. Is this the right hand signal to use? Yes/No

4 You're looking for somewhere to pitch your tent and you spot a river valley (a *wadi*). It looks nice and level, and sheltered from the wind.

But is it really a safe place to camp? Yes/No

5 Your camel's playing up something rotten and you ask a local Bedouin camel herder for help. He tells you to pour spit down your camel's nose. But your camel's got a terrible temper and goodness knows what it'll do to you if you try.

Do you dare to follow the Bedouin's advice? Yes/No

6 The worst thing that could happen has happened. You've run out of water and you've still got miles and miles to go. You come across a Tuareg camp and stop to ask for supplies. You've learnt a bit of the local language and decide to try it out. Which word do you use for water? Would 'amise' do the trick? Yes/No

7 Oh dear, you're not having a very good day. You're out of suncream and your delicate skin is starting to burn. It'll be days before you reach a town where you can stock up on supplies. What can you use instead?

Would rubbing your skin with a watermelon work? Yes/No

Answers:

1 Yes. (Skip this next bit if you're squeamish.) This frog might save your life. It survives dry spells by storing water in its skin and sitting it out underground. Local Aborigines trick the frogs into croaking by stamping their feet on the ground. The stamping sounds to the frog like thunder which might mean rain!

Then the Aborigines dig the frogs up, hold them over their mouths and squeeeeeeze!

2 No. The best thing to do in a dust or sandstorm is crouch down next to your camel and cover your face and mouth. That's where a Tuareg veil comes in handy. If you stand up and try to brave it out, you'll be blown away or end up having stinging sand kicked in your face. Painful.

3 No. That's the signal for a duck, silly. And ducks don't scare anybody. By the time you've realized your mistake, it could be too late. The lion will have had you for lunch. Here's the signal you should have used.

4 No. Learn a lesson from the locals and never pitch your tent in a *wadi*. Whatever you do. It might look very inviting at the moment but all that could change if it starts to rain. One minute, the *wadi*'s nice and dry, the next it's a raging torrent. Flash floods can happen at any time and the ground simply can't soak up the overflow. So it pours down the *wadi*. You won't have time to call for help. You'll already have been swept away.

5 Yes. Your camel's probably been plagued by evil spirits. And the ancient Bedouin cure for this is to pour a mixture of water and camel spit down its nose. It's guaranteed to turn your camel into … a … er pussycat. But mind your camel doesn't try to bite you. I mean, how would you like having spit poured down your nose?

6 No. You'll have to try again. In the Tuareg language "amise" means camel. The word for water is "aman". But make sure you've got something to give the Tuareg in return for the water. Never go empty-handed. Sugar cubes always go down well (for making Tuareg tea, of course).

7 Yes. Believe it or not, it will work nicely. Instead of suncream, the San crush up some roasted watermelon seeds and mash them into a pulp. It's brilliant at protecting their skin from the sun. Of course, it might also make you irresistible to insects, especially if they've got a sweet tooth…

Now add up your teacher's score…

He gets one point for each right answer. How did he do?

Score: 0–2. Oh dear! Your teacher's brain seems to have wilted in the heat. His common sense seems to have utterly deserted him.

Score: 3–5. Not bad! Your teacher has kept his wits about him and not got too bogged down in the sand. But that looks like a nasty camel bite. How on Earth did he get it?

Score: 6–7. Congratulations! Your teacher's survived! (Now don't all cheer at once!) Why not enter him in the next Mr Desert Competition? It's held every year in the Thar Desert, India. He'll need to do well in five categories: moustache-growing (the longer and curlier, the better),

turban-tying (against the clock),

public speaking (last year's winning speech was called "Why I like the desert so much", cringe),

camel-racing (over 500 metres) and, finally, camel fancy dress.

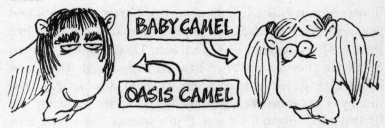

BABY CAMEL

OASIS CAMEL

Do you think your teacher has got what it takes to win the Mr Desert crown?

So, armed with loads of local knowledge, you've packed your teacher off to the desperate desert and you're looking forward to a few days off. Don't worry, he'll be following in well-trodden footsteps. Not only have local people lived in deserts for centuries, hundreds of intrepid explorers have also set off to find out what all the fuss was about. Some have even lived to tell the tale. (Some have never been seen again.) For others, though, it was a case of out of the frying pan and into the fire. If you get my drift...

People have been exploring the deserts for centuries. They've been blasted by sandstorms, bitten by camels and generally fried alive. Some have gone mad, or bad or lost their cool. Many have ended up lost. Dead lost. So why on Earth did they do it? Why put their lives at risk when they could have stayed in bed? Some of them were in it for the money. They wanted to open the desert up for trade. Others had no good reason for going. It just seemed like a good idea at the time. An adventure of a lifetime. They had no idea what lay in store. Some, like your teacher, studied how the local people coped and copied their age-old desert skills. Which greatly improved their chances of survival. Fancy a horrible holiday?

Horrible Holidays are proud to present their

SENSATIONAL SAHARAN SAFARI

Fed up with ordinary caravan holidays?

1000 KM TO NOWHERE

Tired of squabbles about who gets the best bunk?

Had enough of sitting indoors in the rain?

BOOK YOUR PLACE TODAY

For a caravan holiday with a difference, book now on our deadly desert tour. (Better still, get your parents to pay.) Wave goodbye to crowded caravan sites, damp fields and traffic jams. Forget all about being squashed in a small space and those irritating cupboards that never stay shut. Time to get away from it all. Sleep under the stars in a luxury tent and soak up the age-old atmosphere of dreamy Timbuktu. It's the holiday that'll bring out the nomad in you.

Maximum 100 camels per caravan. (In the past, camel caravans travelling through the Sahara have been up to 1,800 strong).

HOW DO I SLEEP ON ONE OF THESE ?

Led by expert Tuareg guides. (They've been leading camel caravans across the Sahara for hundreds of years.)

Tried and tested transport. (Caravans have been used for centuries to carry people and goods across the Sahara. The goods included dates, salt and gold which were carried to market to trade. The people included local traders and intrepid explorers – remember René Caillié? – who came along for the ride.)

What one satisfied customer said:

"It was brilliant. I got on really well with my camel. It only bit me once or twice. I'll never go in an ordinary caravan ever again."

Small print: Our caravans are hand-picked for your comfort. But you won't find mod cons like hot showers, central heating or tellies on board. If you can't live without them, we suggest you try our brand-new Couch Potato Tour. Coming soon to a sofa near you.

Desperate desert fact file

NAME: Australian Desert

LOCATION: Australia

SIZE: 3,800,000 sq km

TEMPERATURE: Hot summers up to 53°C; cold winters down to −4°C

RAINFALL: Less than 100 mm a year

DESERT TYPE: High pressure; rain shadow

DESERT DATA:

- Two-thirds of Australia is desperate desert.
- This is made up of the Simpson, Great Sandy, Great Victoria and Tanami deserts.
- Uluru is a huge red rock worn away by the desert wind. It's sacred to the Aborigine people.
- The largest desert lake is Lake Eyre. It filled for the first time on record in 1950.

Crossing Australia, by camel

The Sahara is not the only desert where camels have come in handy. In 1860, two intrepid explorers, Robert O'Hara Burke and William John Wills, set off to cross Australia from south to north. It was one of the most daring expeditions ever. For years, people had wondered what lay in the middle of Australia. According to rumour it was either a great inland lake, or a huge, parched desert, bone-dry and baking hot. (In fact, the latter turned out to be true, as they would have known if they'd only bothered to ask the local Aborigine people who'd been living there for thousands of years. They knew every inch of the desert, and where to find precious food and water.) Anyway, just in case it was a desert, they took along some camels for the ride.

20 August 1860, Melbourne, Australia

When Burke and Wills set out from Melbourne on 20 August 1860, their camels were the talk of the town. The crowds who came to cheer the men on their way had never seen anything like them before. Some onlookers screamed. Others fainted. Others simply stood and stared. The camels had been brought over from India especially for this expedition and they were certainly causing a stir.

The expedition had taken months to plan. It was the largest and costliest ever seen in Australia. And it had already been a rocky road. Burke was brave and charming, it was true, but he was also horribly bad-tempered. He flew off the handle at anything.

(Secretly, it was said that bolshy Burke only applied for the job because he'd been unlucky in love. Or was it the large cash prize?) To make matters worse, Burke had no experience of exploration (he'd been a police officer before) nor of living in the bush. (And he wasn't the sort of man to think the locals could teach him anything.) Wills, on the other hand, was quietly spoken, loyal and dependable, and got on brilliantly with everyone.

Which was just as well. Just a few weeks into the trip, Burke sacked his deputy and gave the job to Wills.

There was no time to lose. They weren't the only ones making the journey. The great explorer, John McDouall Stuart, had already set out from Adelaide with a good few months' head start on them. But Burke had no intention of finishing second. No intention at all. So apart from being horribly high-handed and headstrong, he was also a man in a hurry. Did they make it? What did they find? Did Burke eventually swallow his pride and consult the local Aborigine people? Where better to look for the answers than in long-suffering Wills' expedition diary? (His real diary didn't go quite like this but it did give us most of the information we have about the jinxed journey.)

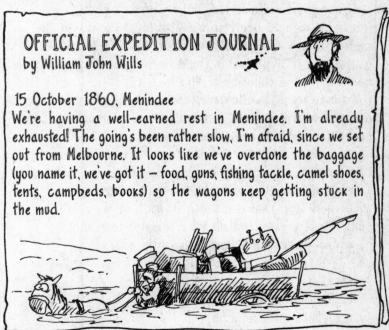

OFFICIAL EXPEDITION JOURNAL
by William John Wills

15 October 1860, Menindee

We're having a well-earned rest in Menindee. I'm already exhausted! The going's been rather slow, I'm afraid, since we set out from Melbourne. It looks like we've overdone the baggage (you name it, we've got it – food, guns, fishing tackle, camel shoes, tents, campbeds, books) so the wagons keep getting stuck in the mud.

(Not a desert in sight so far. The first part of the journey has taken us over muddy farmland through the pouring rain!) And those pesky camels keep frightening the horses.

Menindee's a tumbledown sort of place and Mr Burke doesn't want to hang around long. Can't say I blame him. Trouble is, summer's coming and it's already really too hot to carry on. Anyway, Mr Burke's decided that a group of us (Mr Burke, King, Brahe, Gray, Wright and myself) will press on with some of the camels and horses to Cooper Creek. The others will follow later with the rest of the supplies — we hope.

(Note: In Australia, the seasons are the other way round.)

me

11 November 1860, Cooper Creek

I can't believe it. We've reached Cooper Creek at last. Thank goodness. Only 650 long, hard kilometres to get here. Wright's gone back to Menindee to fetch the others. The rest of us are too tired to do anything. Whoever warned us not to travel in summer was right — the heat has been terrible.

At first sight, this is a delightful spot, with a cool river and lots of pretty (and shady) eucalyptus trees. And even though we seem to have reached the edge of a desert, there are birds and fish everywhere — heaven! Or so we thought... But we've had to hang our supplies on strings in

118

the trees. Why? Because otherwise the bloomin' rats will eat them. (I hate rats.) Oh, I forgot to mention — it's 43°C in the shade. I'm boiling. Will I ever get used to it? Now all we can do is wait for Mr Wright to return.

15 December 1860, Cooper Creek
Still here, I'm afraid. Wright's not back and Mr Burke is restless. That Stuart's really getting to him. So we (Mr Burke, King, Gray and me) are leaving tomorrow. We're making a dash for the Gulf of Carpentaria, the northernmost point of our journey.

I'm not looking forward to it. (Don't tell the others.) It's 2,400 kilometres there and back again, and guess what, we're walking all the way. I'm going to have blisters on my blisters! We're taking Mr Burke's horse and six of the camels, but not to carry us — worse luck. They'll carry the food (dried horsemeat) and water. We'll carry out our own guns and bedrolls. We're not taking tents. Apparently you don't need tents in the desert!

Mr B's told the others we'll be back in three months and to wait for us here. Lucky one of us is being optimistic.

our tents!

11 February 1861, the Gulf of Carpentaria (almost)
We've made it! It's been a dreadful journey and I can't believe I'm still here to write this diary. We walked and walked for 11 hours a day, every day, through blistering heat, thick swarms of flies and choking sandstorms. Real desert weather. (You can

imagine how bad-tempered that made the camels.) All we had to eat were a few bits of that old dried horsemeat I mentioned and a handful of boiled plants. Apparently, they're called portulaca. Give me a nice juicy chop any day.

In January, the rains began and the ground turned into a mud bath. We travelled by night when it was a bit cooler – though it made it a bit difficult to see where we were going. Today, Mr Burke and I tried to reach the sea. It's only a few kilometres off. But wouldn't you know it – a pesky mangrove swamp forced us back. It was bitterly disappointing. Still, as Mr B says, at least we got further than that fool, Stuart (Mr B's words, not mine).

17 April 1861, Goodness knows where
What a rotten day! For days Gray's been complaining about feeling ill. But we all thought he was faking. (Anything to get out of carrying his own bed roll.) I mean, we're all exhausted and half-starved, not just him. So imagine our horror when we found him ... dead!

It took all day to bury him because we were so weak. The journey back from the coast has been a nightmare. It's rained non-stop since we left, and we've had to sleep out in the wet. (What was that about not needing tents?) We've run out of rations and our clothes are in rags. We managed to catch a snake to eat (and I'm afraid we had to eat four of the camels). But I don't know how long we can go on like this...

21 April 1861, Cooper Creek
I could have cried with joy when we arrived back at the camp this evening. But my happiness was short-lived. The others have gone. GONE! The camp's deserted. All that was left of them was a note pinned to a tree, showing us a place to dig. So we started digging, what else could we do?

Eventually, we unearthed a box with one month's rations inside and a scribbled note from Brahe. Would you believe it? They only left this morning. Just a few hours ago!
Brahe's heading back to Menindee. And who can blame him? He waited a whole four months for us to get back. But we're all too exhausted to go after him. We'll set out for Mount Hopeless tomorrow and try to reach the police station there. It seems like the only thing we can do.

27 June 1861, Cooper Creek

This is terrible. We can't go on for much longer. We've been going round in circles for days, getting nowhere. All our food and water is used up and there's only one camel left between us. (The other one got stuck in the mud so we shot it.) Things are looking pretty desperate now. Some friendly locals gave us some fish to eat — they have little enough to eat themselves.

But then they were on the way again. Can't say I blame them. If only we'd asked for their help before. Things might have been so different. I've written a letter to my father telling him what has happened. It might be my last. Unless we're rescued soon, we'll starve to death...

Signed W. J. Wills *W. J. Wills*

A very sad ending

If you're easily upset, skip this next bit or have your hanky handy. Two days later, Burke and King left the camp for the last time to look for help. Brave old Burke died on the way of starvation and exposure. When King got back to the camp, he found that Wills was also dead. King spent three months living with a group of Aborigines who took pity on him. When he was rescued, he was ragged, starving and half mad. Wills' (real) journal was found next to his skeleton.

It was a tragic ending. And it could all have been so different. If only heroic Burke and Wills had reached Cooper Creek just eight short hours earlier…

Desert exploration awards

To … sniff … cheer you up … sniff … a bit, the *Daily Globe* asked readers to vote for their top desert explorers. And here's Sandy to announce the results. Welcome to the Explorer Oscars.

MOST INTREPID EXPLORER (Male)

Runner-up

German geographer and explorer, Heinrich Barth (1821–1865) spent five years surviving in the Sahara. He spent six months living in Timbuktu, learning desert-craft from the locals. Heinrich was gone so long, he was given up for dead and his obituary was published in the paper. Then in August 1855, he emerged from the desert hale and hearty, with camel-loads of notes. Unfortunately he was so unpopular that no one really cared two hoots.

And the winner is…

In 1886, British soldier and explorer, Francis Younghusband (1863–1942), crossed the Gobi simply because it was there. All he took with him was a local guide, two porters, eight camels and a large supply of sherry.

What a guy! What's more he made it, covering 2,000 kilometres in 70 days. Was that it? Was it heck. After four days' rest, fearless Francis was off again, this time across the desperate Takla Makan. An outstanding performance.

MOST INTREPID EXPLORER (Female)

Runner-up

English explorer and writer, Gertrude Bell (1868–1926), comes second in this category. Frightfully posh Gertrude left behind a glittering social life in London and Europe to travel across the Arabian Desert. Of course, old habits die hard and even in the desert she always remembered her manners. She always dressed neatly in a nice dress and hat, and had the table laid with the best silver for dinner.

And the winners are…

Misses Mildred Cable, Eva French and Francesca French share this year's top award. A life of cream teas and croquet was not for these three plucky ladies. They spent years in China working as missionaries. Then, in 1926, they travelled across the Gobi Desert by mule-cart, accompanied by two saucepans, a cake tin, two jugs and a stove.

Only then did our heroines return to England, retire to a cottage in the country and write their book about the extraordinary places they'd seen and the people they'd met.

LUCKIEST TO BE ALIVE (In any category)
Runner-up
In 1894, Swede Sven Hedin (1865–1952) insisted on trying to cross the Taklan Makan, even though the local people warned him not to go.

He made it but he nearly died of thirst on the way. When his water ran out, with days of walking still to go, he survived by drinking chicken blood (he'd taken the chickens along for food). Later he gave a lecture in America about his murderous "March of Death". It made his audience so desperately thirsty they rushed out in droves for a drink!

And the winner is…

A unanimous decision. In 1844, Australian Charles Sturt (1795–1869), set off to explore the deserted middle of Australia. Unluckily for him, it was a desperately hot summer. So hot that all the waterholes dried up. Sturt got scurvy, almost went blind and could hardly walk. When he got home, two years later, his wife fainted when she opened the door. She'd given him up for dead.

Modern-day exploration

Feeling restless? Bored of sitting around at home? If all of this has given you a taste for adventure, why not set off to explore the desert for yourself?

If camels aren't your cup of tea, there are lots of other ways of travelling. You can go by car, or truck or motorbike. Either way, you'll be in good company. Each year, 100 dare-devil drivers take part in the perilous Paris–Dakar Rally, straight across the scorching Sahara. The desert bit of the journey takes about three days. But don't expect to find nice straight roads and handy road signs to guide you over the sand dunes. You'll have to navigate by satellite. Even then, it's easy to take a wrong turn. Dead easy. Despite several trial runs and an official guidebook, many drivers still get horribly lost.

And if that's not desperate enough for you, how about signing up for the strength-sapping Marathon des Sables. (If you want to know what that means, see what Sandy's got to say on the next page.) Be warned – this is seriously strenuous stuff. Not for the faint-hearted. Is it really that gruelling? Yes, it is. Have you ever tried to run in sand? It's impossible to get a firm grip with your feet so you're constantly slipping and sliding.

THIS MUST BE SOME BONE HE'S BURYING!

You have to run 225 kilometres over the sandy Sahara (in six stages). The good news is that you've got six days to do it in. The bad news is that you'll be running in temperatures of up to 58°C. You'll have to carry a 10-kilogram rucksack (that's like lugging around ten bags of sugar on your back) with your food, water and bed inside. And you'll need to wear shoes two sizes too big because your feet will swell up like balloons in the heat. (You'll also need to hold your nose when you take your shoes off. Phwoar!) Not to mention the blisters. Still keen?

WOW! HIS FEET MUST REALLY SWELL!

That's French for Marathon of the Sands. But don't let that fool you. Just because it's got a fancy French name, it doesn't make it any less exhausting. And don't even think about cheating by getting a head start. You're only told the route the night before! Give me a camel any day!

WISE WORDS!

Earth-shattering fact

For the latest in desperate desert transport, you'll need to set your sights on outer space. The Lunar Rover was used by the American Apollo astronauts to explore the moon. But where was it tested? In the Californian desert, of course. It's the closest landscape to the moon we've got.

If you must head off into the desperate desert, always take some company. Never ever travel alone. There'll be no one to go for help if you run into trouble. A local guide is your best bet. Stick with them and you might just stand a chance. What? You've changed your mind about going? Well, I must say I'm glad. No point getting all hot and bothered for nothing. Why not have a well-earned rest and get to know the other side of the desert? The side that's horribly useful...

SPOILSPORT

DESERT TREASURE

What on Earth can you use a desperate desert for? You might think nothing at all. I mean, deserts are just a load of useless old rocks scattered about in the sand, aren't they? But looks can be deceptive. If you scratch the surface of the desert, you might get a surprise. Buried beneath the sand are some horribly useful desert spoils. It's just a case of knowing where to find them. Here are five things you might not expect to find in the desperate desert:

1 Life-saving salt. Salt isn't just tasty when it's sprinkled on chips, it can actually save your life. It's true! Believe it or not, your body needs eight tablespoons of salt every day to stay alive. It keeps your body in working order. Normally, you get most of this salt from the food you eat. In the desperate desert heat, though, you lose spoonfuls of salt when you sweat. Luckily, there's plenty more around. Salt's been mined in the desert for thousands of years. Here's what happens:

- A rare downpour of rain fills a dried-up lake.
- The water sucks up salt from the soil (desert soil's seriously salty).
- Then the water evaporates in the sun…
- … leaving a thick layer of life-saving salt.
- Miners use long poles to prise up huge slabs of salt. They cut the salty slabs into bricks.

- The bricks are sold to traders, loaded on camels and carried off across the desert ...
- ... to a special salt market. Here the salt's sold or swapped for tea, sugar or gold.

If this sounds too tiring, try a more restful remedy. Simply dissolve a salt tablet in a glass of water and slurp that down instead. (Drink it quickly – it tastes horrible!)

2 Oodles of oil. Oil is the most valuable desert spoil and there's barrels of the stuff under the desert. But how on Earth did it get there? Well, millions of years ago, the deserts were covered in swampy forests and seas.

When the plants and animals died, their bodies rotted and were buried under layers of rock. Which squashed them up into thick, gungy oil. Clever, eh? But you have to dig deep to get the oil out. Then it's pumped out of the ground and piped across the desert to an oil refinery. About a quarter of all the oil we use comes from the b-oil-ing Arabian Desert...

Desperate desert fact file

NAME: Arabian Desert

LOCATION: The Middle East

SIZE: 2,600,000 sq km

TEMPERATURE: Hot summers up to 54°C; cold winters down to −3°C

RAINFALL: Less than 100 mm

DESERT TYPE: High pressure

DESERT DATA:

● Oil was first struck in the 1930s. And it has made countries like Saudi Arabia seriously rich.

● Fierce winds called shamals blow twice a year whipping up tonnes of dust and sand.

● In 1950, temperatures fell to −12°C, with several centimetres of ice and snow. Brrr!

● Millions of Muslim pilgrims flock to the desert every year to visit the holy city of Mecca.

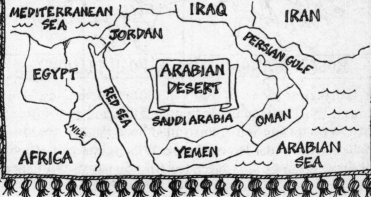

3 Dazzling diamonds. Diamonds in the desert? Sounds too good to be true? To see for yourself, head for the desperate Namib Desert. Hidden under its shifting sand dunes are dozens of dazzling diamonds. They formed tens of millions of years ago when the chemical carbon, in underground rocks, was heated to an incredibly high temperature by a volcanic eruption. Yes, things were very different in the desert tens of millions of years ago. Then the carbon cooled down and formed diamonds. Of course, diamonds don't look all posh and sparkly to start off with. (Well, would you if you were millions of years old?) They're buried under tonnes of gravel and dust. This is dug up and sent to a processing plant where all the gorgeous gemstones are sifted out. And it doesn't stop at diamonds. Gold (remember the story of gold–digging Pablo Valencia?), silver, opals, copper and iron are all to be found in deserts.

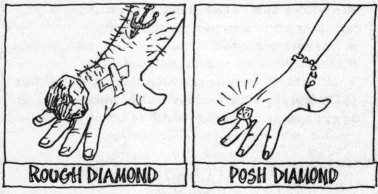

ROUGH DIAMOND   POSH DIAMOND

4 Glittering glass. If you can't afford diamonds, don't worry. What about a lovely lump of glittering glass instead? Just as pretty and won't cost you a thing. Parts of the sandy Sahara are covered in chunks of greeny-yellow glass. (Some of these chunks are soccer-ball sized.) Scientists think there may be 1,400 TONNES of the stuff scattered around the Sahara (so a tiny weeny lump shouldn't be missed). But where on Earth did all this glass come from? One theory is that, millions of years ago, a massive meteorite smashed into the Earth and melted tonnes and tonnes of sand. Then the sand cooled and turned into solid glass. Sounds reasonable!

5 Economy electricity. One thing you'll find plenty of in the desert is sunshine. The sun's in your face almost all day long. It's hot and it's also horribly useful. How? Well, at a solar power station, the sunlight falls on solar cells (like the ones you get in your solar-powered calculator) and is turned into electricity. It can be used to pump water from underground and heat water for people's homes. It's cheap, it's clean and it won't run out. And horrible geographers can't get enough of it! The largest solar-power station in the world is in the Mojave Desert in California.

Earth-shattering fact
If it's art you're after, head for the desert. The Nazca Desert in Peru. The ground is covered in patterns of lines and animal pictures, drawn about 5,000 years ago. (To get a good view, you'll need to stand on top of a hill. The pictures are enormous.) No one really knows why they're there. Some experts think they're a gigantic astrological chart, used for telling the future. Others claim they were runways for alien spacecraft. Weird.

How green is your desert?
The deserted desert's probably the last place you'd expect to find lush green fields. But farmers have been growing crops in the desert for thousands of years. So how do you turn

bone-dry desert into fabulously fertile farmland? (The posh name for this is irrigation.) The answer is, you've guessed it, water! Buckets and buckets of water. And in the desert, it's easier said than done. If you were a desperate desert farmer, how would you water your fields? Decide which method you think works best, then check out the answers on pages 138–9. Here's Sandy to show you how it's done.

1 Dig a *qanat*. A *qanat* (kha–nat) is a man-made water tunnel dug deep under the ground. Here's how it works:

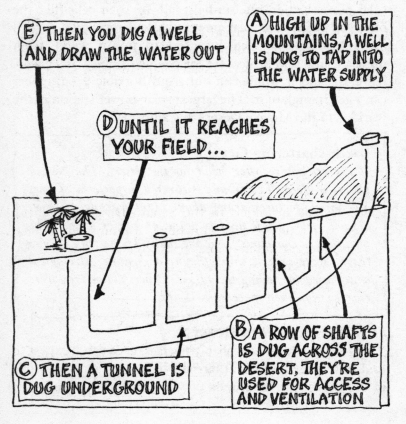

E THEN YOU DIG A WELL AND DRAW THE WATER OUT

A HIGH UP IN THE MOUNTAINS, A WELL IS DUG TO TAP INTO THE WATER SUPPLY

D UNTIL IT REACHES YOUR FIELD...

B A ROW OF SHAFTS IS DUG ACROSS THE DESERT, THEY'RE USED FOR ACCESS AND VENTILATION

C THEN A TUNNEL IS DUG UNDERGROUND

2 Build a wall. Rain rarely falls in the Negev Desert in Israel. (Its name means "to dry".) So farmers have to make the most of even the diddiest downpour. They build low stone walls around their fields. The walls trap water which flows along channels into the fields.

3 Cover them with plastic. In the Negev again, you sometimes see fields full of plastic bags! It's true! No, you haven't gone mad. The bags are there to make sure your plants stay well watered.

4 Use a giant sprinkler. In the Sahara Desert in Libya, farmers water their fields with huge, spinning sprinklers. The sprinklers are fixed to long arms which move round the field like the hands on a clock. Tick, tock. They use water pumped from deep underground.

137

1 You'll be in good company if you choose this one. This really ingenious irrigation idea was first used by ancient Persian farmers 7,000 years ago. Want to know the best thing about it? Because the water flows underground, it doesn't evaporate and it stays ice cold. Cool, eh? In fact, qanats are so horribly clever they're still used today in Iran, the Middle East and China.

2 Another tried and tested method. The old ones are often the best, I always say. This one was first thought up 2,000 years ago. Recently it's been revived by farmers wanting to turn the desert green. And it's been such a bloomin' brilliant success that they've been able to grow peaches, almonds, wheat and tomatoes.

3 A simple but successful solution. Here's what you do. You lay a long pipe on the ground and plant your plants along them. Then you cover the whole thing in plastic. Let a steady trickle of water flow along the pipe to wet the plants at their roots. What's the plastic for? Well, it stops the water evaporating away in the sun.

4 A very good choice. Forget hose pipes and watering cans. Using these seriously sophisticated sprinklers, farmers have created huge wheatfields half a mile wide. They look like giant green saucers in the sand. The whole thing is controlled by computer.

So, which works best? Actually, they all do! And now that you've turned the dusty desert into farmland, here are some of the things you could grow...

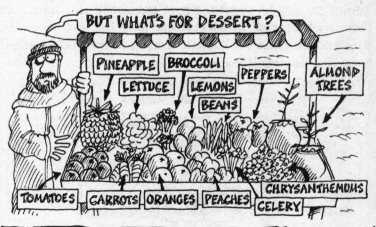

BUT WHAT'S FOR DESSERT?

PINEAPPLE · BROCCOLI · LETTUCE · LEMONS · BEANS · PEPPERS · ALMOND TREES · TOMATOES · CARROTS · ORANGES · PEACHES · CHRYSANTHEMUMS · CELERY

Earth-shattering fact

You know the saying "money doesn't grow on trees"? Well, money might not but plastic does. Honestly! And it's all down to a desert wildflower (OK so it's not exactly a tree) called popweed. Its oily sap can be turned into plastic for making things like toys, shoes and bits of cars. Might be worth planting a field or two?

139

Desperate desert cities

Fancy living in a place where the sun always shines, where there's loads of fresh air and wide, open spaces? Fancy living in the desperate desert?

You might not be able to wait to get out of the desert but there are plenty of others ready to move in. Take Phoenix, Arizona, for example. It's smack bang in the middle of the bone-dry Sonoran Desert.

Cities like it are springing up all over the desert especially in the USA and Australia. To keep a city like this going, you need about 76 BILLION gallons of water a year. That's an unbelievable number of buckets! So where does all this water come from? Some cities pump it from underground. Others bring it by pipe from far-off rivers.

SAND DUNE & CACTUS

ESTATE AGENTS

HELPING YOU GET AWAY FROM IT ALL

FOR SALE

House with large garden and swimming pool...

CALIFORNIA

NEVADA

UTAH

MEXICO

LOCATION: PHOENIX ARIZONA, USA
A PRIME DESERT SITE

SPECIAL FEATURES:
THE HOUSE COMES WITH AIR-CONDITIONING SO YOU CAN ENJOY THE WARMTH WITHOUT IT FRYING YOUR BRAIN. GREAT VIEWS OVER THE DESERT - ON A CLEAR DAY (AND IT'S ALWAYS A CLEAR DAY IN THE DESERT) YOU CAN SEE FOR MILES AND MILES

HAVE A NICE DAY, Y'ALL

SMALL PRINT

YOUR WATER SUPPLY COMES FROM THE COLORADO RIVER. IT'S BROUGHT BY PIPE STRAIGHT TO YOUR HOME.
SO MUCH WATER'S BEEN TAKEN FROM THE RIVER THAT IT'S RUNNING DRY.
EXPECT WATER SHORTAGES IN THE FUTURE.

Living in the desert has never been easier. But there's a horribly high price to pay. It's not just the rivers that are drying up. Horrible humans have been using up so much underground water, it could soon all be gone. Trouble is, some of it's been there for thousands of years. And it'll take thousands more to refill. So you could be waiting some time for a shower. Shame. And that's not all...

DESERTS IN DANGER

Using up all the water is one thing. But deserts are facing a deadlier danger – they seem to be on the move! All over the world, deserts are spreading. You might not think it's much of a problem. I mean, what difference would a bit more desert make? Well, it isn't a problem for the deserts. But for people living on the edge of some of the world's deserts, it can be a desperate situation. Turning a desert into fertile farmland is a horribly costly business. Many people have to scratch a living in fields at the desert edge. It's tough at the best of times. But if the desert grows and turns these fields into useless dust, they'll have nowhere to grow their crops. And no crops means no food. And that would be disastrous.

Deadly desertification

So why on Earth are deserts fraying at the edges? What's causing this deadly spread? Even horrible geographers can't agree. So we sent Sandy to try to dig up some answers…

"DESERT SPREAD" DOESN'T SOUND VERY POSH, DOES IT?

NOPE, IT DOESN'T. TECHNICALLY, HORRIBLE GEOGRAPHERS CALL WHAT'S HAPPENING DESERTIFICATION. IT'S BORING, I KNOW, BUT YOU GET THEIR DRIFT. THEY AGREE THAT IT MEANS HOW A DESERT IS MADE. SO FAR, SO GOOD. MIND YOU, THEY DISAGREE ABOUT ALMOST EVERYTHING ELSE.

I SEE. SO WHAT ACTUALLY HAPPENS THEN?

MOST GEOGRAPHERS THINK IT GOES SOMETHING LIKE THIS. ONE WAY OR ANOTHER, THE LAND AT THE EDGES OF THE DESERT TURNS TO DUST WHICH IS EASILY BLOWN AWAY BY THE WIND, OR WASHED AWAY BY RARE BURSTS OF RAINFALL.

CAN THIS HAPPEN NATURALLY?

YES, IT CAN. TINY CHANGES IN THE EARTH'S ORBIT AROUND THE SUN (THAT'S THE WAY THE EARTH TRAVELS AROUND THE SUN) CAN ALTER THE EARTH'S WEATHER. IF IT TURNS WINDIER AND DRIER THAN NORMAL, THERE'S TROUBLE AHEAD. THE LAND DRIES OUT AND TURNS TO DUST, AND YOU KNOW THE REST.

HAVE PEOPLE MADE MATTERS WORSE?

UNFORTUNATELY, THEY HAVE. USING THE SAME LAND OVER AND OVER AGAIN TO GROW CROPS DOESN'T GIVE IT ENOUGH TIME TO RECOVER. ALSO, TOO MANY SHEEP AND GOATS GOBBLE UP TOO MUCH GRASS, AND TOO MANY TREES ARE CHOPPED DOWN FOR FIREWOOD.

BUT HOW ON EARTH DOES THIS MAKE A DESERT?

WELL, THE CROPS SUCK UP GOODNESS FROM THE SOIL, LEAVING IT DRIED UP AND DEAD. YOU SEE? AND WITHOUT ANY PLANT ROOTS TO CEMENT THE SOIL TOGETHER, IT'S EASILY BLOWN AWAY. ALSO, ANY WATER WASHES STRAIGHT OFF THE SOIL INSTEAD OF SOAKING IN. WELCOME TO THE DESERT.

SO PEOPLE ARE REALLY TO BLAME, THEN?

YES AND NO. THE THING IS THAT PEOPLE HAVE TO GROW CROPS FOR FOOD, OR THEY'LL STARVE. BUT THE POPULATION'S GROWING SO FAST THAT THE LAND CAN'T TAKE THE PRESSURE. TROUBLE IS, IF THE LAND TURNS TO DESERT, PEOPLE WILL STARVE ANYWAY. IT'S A VERY VICIOUS CIRCLE.

HOW MUCH NEW DESERT ARE WE TALKING ABOUT?

SOME GEOGRAPHERS THINK THAT ABOUT 100 SQ KM OF LAND IS TURNING TO DUST EVERY DAY! (THAT'S ABOUT THE SAME AS TEN FULL-SIZED SOCCER PITCHES.) SPELLING DISASTER FOR ABOUT 900 MILLION PEOPLE. THAT'S ABOUT A SIXTH OF THE WORLD'S POPULATION.

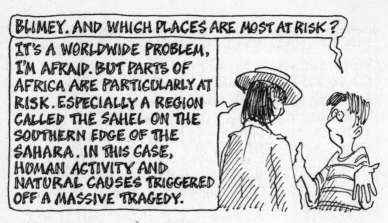

BLIMEY. AND WHICH PLACES ARE MOST AT RISK?

IT'S A WORLDWIDE PROBLEM, I'M AFRAID. BUT PARTS OF AFRICA ARE PARTICULARLY AT RISK. ESPECIALLY A REGION CALLED THE SAHEL ON THE SOUTHERN EDGE OF THE SAHARA. IN THIS CASE, HUMAN ACTIVITY AND NATURAL CAUSES TRIGGERED OFF A MASSIVE TRAGEDY.

The Sahel, Africa, 1984–1985

In 1984–1985, the Sahel suffered one of the worst droughts ever to strike Africa. Very little rain falls in this part of the world normally. But this year, the rains completely failed. With no water, the land quickly turned to dust. The local farmers watched helplessly as their precious crops withered and died.

There was nothing they could do. But worse was to come. Without any food to eat, people began to starve to death. In the dreadful famine that followed, almost a million people died of hunger and disease. In Ethiopia alone, about half the country's cattle starved to death. All over the region, desperate villagers left their homes and farms in search of food and water. Millions ended up sheltering in refugee camps and feeding centres set up to help the victims. Some had walked for days. They were homeless, hungry and terrified. Worst of all, no one knew how long their nightmare would last.

The word Sahel means shore. But not the sort of shore you'd find by the sea. It describes the strip of land along the southern edge of the vast Sahara Desert. The Sahel stretches for 500 kilometres from Senegal and Mauritania on the west coast, to Sudan and Ethiopia in the east, and covers about a fifth of Africa.

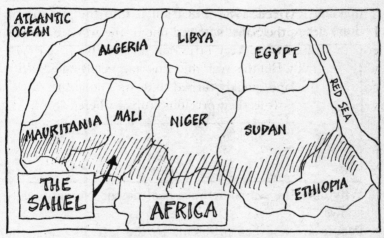

For eight months of the year, between October and June, the Sahel is bone dry. But there are a few rainy months between June and September. During this time, enough rain usually falls for farmers to grow their crops and raise their animals. Usually. But not this time. This time there was no rain. And it caused a catastrophe. And it wasn't the first time. Devastating droughts had already struck the Sahel in the 1960s and 1970s.

So why on Earth did this terrible tragedy happen?

- Put simply, drought means a lack of rainfall which can last for months or even years. It's the usual state of things in the desert. The problems start if a drought comes unexpectedly or lasts longer than usual. Then it can be disastrous.

- The Sahel has suffered droughts on and off for the last 40 years. So what on Earth makes it so drought-prone? Some geographers blame the Atlantic Ocean (off the western end of the Sahel). But how can a sea possibly be to blame? It's all down to temperature. If the sea is cooler than normal, less moisture rises from it into the air, so you don't get rain clouds forming.

Why does the sea sometimes cool down? Nobody really knows.

- People are another problem. In the last 50 years, the Sahel's population has grown very quickly, thanks to a few years of really heavy rain. With more mouths to feed, farmers had to grow more crops more quickly. Which put the land under pressure. It never had time to recover. In the past, it was left for 15–20 years before being farmed again. Now it was used within five years.

- And it doesn't stop there. We use technology to make life easier, but in the Sahel it made things worse. New equipment meant people could dig deeper wells. Which meant they could keep more animals. Which ate all the plants, so the soil dried up and, well, you know the rest. In the Sahel, staying alive is a horribly delicate balance.

- When the land turns to dust and blows away, where on Earth does it go? Into the awesome atmosphere, of course.

Where it too can actually reduce the chances of rain. How? Well, a thick, choking dollop of dust stops the air moving so it can't cool and condense into clouds. So even the dust stirred up during a drought adds to the problem. Pretty desperate, really.

Horrible Health Warning

And it's not just deserts that are drying up. The Aral Sea is, too. (Actually it isn't a real sea. It's a salty inland lake. It's just called a sea. See?) The arid Aral lies in the middle of the Turkestan Desert (see page 150). And for the past 14,000 years, it has relied on two large rivers to fill it with water. But not any more. Now so much water has been piped from the rivers for irrigation and drinking that the Aral Sea is shrinking. Between 1960 and 1990 it halved in size. And it's still getting smaller. What water's left is now so salty that fish can't survive. And once-busy fishing ports are now left stranded on the shore, miles away from the water.

Desperate desert fact file

NAME: Turkestan Desert
LOCATION: Central Asia
SIZE: 450,000 sq km
TEMPERATURE: Hot summers up to 49°C. Freezing winters down to −42°C
RAINFALL: 70–150 mm
DESERT TYPE: Inland desert
DESERT DATA:

- It's two deserts really – the Kara Kum (Black Sands) and the Kyzyl Kum (Red Sands).
- It's dotted with bare patches of clay called takyrs which are used for collecting water. This means farmers can grow exotic fruit like melons and grapes in the middle of the desert.
- Ninety per cent of the Kara Kum is crisscrossed by greyish-coloured sand dunes, which are hundreds of kilometres long.
- Thirty million years ago, the whole desert was covered in salty sea.

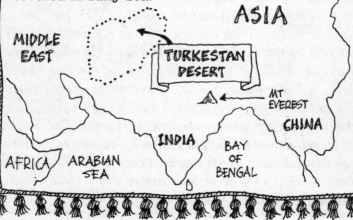

ASIA

MIDDLE EAST

TURKESTAN DESERT

MT EVEREST

CHINA

INDIA

AFRICA

ARABIAN SEA

BAY OF BENGAL

Stopping the spread

Deserts are horribly sensitive. One false move, and before you know it, you've got a full-blown desert disaster on your hands. But is it all doom and gloom? Are the deserts really taking over? What's being done to hold them back? The good news is that people are trying their best to stop the rot. Desert people all over the world are working hard to strand the sand. But it's a horribly tricky, costly business and many desert countries are very poor. They don't have enough money to spend on food let alone on diverting the deserts. It's a desperate dilemma. Here are just a few of the things they're testing out:

1 Planting trees. The tree roots stick into the soil and stop it blowing away so fast. Tough grasses are good for this, too. Besides, the trees also act like windbreaks to slow down the blasting wind. Over the last ten years in Ethiopia, people have planted 500 million hardy eucalyptus and acacia trees. That's an awful lot of digging.

WHEN I SAID LET'S PLANT A TREE, I MEANT OUTSIDE!

2 Soil-stopping stones. In Africa, farmers lay lines of stones across their fields. These stop the rain simply washing away the soil. It's simple but brilliant. In just a few years, farmers can double their harvests and put some grain in store in case drought strikes again.

3 A load of old dung. Here's another age–old way local people have of turning the desert green again. Why not try it for yourself?

What you need:
- Some cow poo
- A spade
- Some grass seeds
- A clothes peg

What you do:

a) Dig a semi–circular hole in the ground. (It seems that this is the shape that works best. But you don't need to be too picky.)

b) Then fill it with the cow poo. (This is where the peg comes in handy.)

c) Sprinkle the seeds on to the poo.

d) Wait for a few months. (You'll soon get used to the smell.)

What you'll see:
Water condenses on to the nice, warm poo and makes the grass seeds sprout. Soon the sand's covered in lush, green grass. Which, by the way, is brilliant for feeding to your cows! (Then just wait a few hours, grab your spade and off you go again.) Don't forget to remove the clothes peg.

4 What's the mat-ter? In the Gobi Desert, people scatter straw mats over the sand dunes to stop them creeping forward. The mats are spread out like the squares on a chess board. They break up the wind's flow which makes it much weaker so it doesn't have enough strength left to shift the sand.

5 An oily option. In Saudi Arabia, shifting sand dunes bury farms and villages, and clog up vital oil pipelines. But what on Earth can be done? One method is to spray the sand with oil (once you've got the pipeline unclogged, of course). It's quick, cheap and it seals the sand and stops it moving. Sounds the perfect solution? There's just one problem. Unfortunately, the oil also kills off precious trees and plants. And that's the last thing you need. Do any especially tough plants survive? Well, there's one...

Earth-shattering fact

If real trees don't work, try planting some plastic palm trees. Yep, plastic. They look just like the real thing but they don't need watering which is very good news. So how on Earth can you beat back the desert with some plastic plants? The theory is that the trees trap moisture in their leaves and stems at night, then slowly release it during the day. In a few years' time, this will cool down the climate so (real) rain clouds can form. Will it work? Nobody has the faintest idea.

HMM, INTERESTING NEW FLAVOUR

CRUNCH!

MUNCH!

A SANDY FUTURE?

So are the deserts really moving? Or is it just another mind-boggling mirage? Here's what the experts have to say. Don't expect the answers to be quick or simple. Horrible geographers hardly ever see eye to eye. Take these two, for instance. They're keeping their heads firmly stuck in the sand. So it's up to you to make your own mind up.

It's all true, the deserts are getting bigger. And things can only get worse. Already, the Sahara's shifting forward by about 6 whole kilometres a year. At this rate, it'll spread right across the Mediterranean and into Spain, Greece and Italy. (Perhaps the Romans were right after all.) And before you know it, you'll have a sand dune knocking at your door... I'm outta here!

I CAN'T STAND EXPERTS

See what I mean? Desperate, isn't it? And it doesn't stop there. Other experts claim that the Sahara Desert isn't growing at all. Actually, they say, it's shrinking! And they've got the photographs (snapped by satellite cameras) as proof.

So there. Confused? It's baffling enough to bake your brains. But that's geography for you. Nothing's ever cut and dried. You never know what's around the next corner, let alone around the next desert. And that's what makes it so horribly exciting.

BLOOMIN' RAINFORESTS

INTRODUCTION

Here's a quick question for you. Is your geography teacher an alien from outer space? (Warning: Think very carefully before you answer unless you *want* to do extra geography homework for the rest of your schooldays.)

On second thoughts, you might be better off keeping your ideas to yourself. Mind you, it can be horribly tricky telling the difference between your teacher and an alien. Your teacher might as well be from outer space for all the sense she makes. Can you understand a word she's saying?

THE FLORA OF THE TROPICAL RAINFOREST IS LARGELY DENDRITIC WITH DENSE SUB-CROWNS OF FOLIAGE

WHO?

MISS

A normal person would simply say, "In the rainforest you can't see the wood for the trees." See what I mean? Obviously your teacher is "barking" mad. But don't be too tough on your crackpot teacher. Horrible geography can be baffling enough for human beings, let alone for aliens with two heads *and* two brains. But just imagine if your teacher really did come from another planet. What on Earth would she make of your weird world? Picture the scene. You're sitting in on double geography on far-off Planet Blob...

161

TODAY'S LESSON IS ALL ABOUT THE PLANET CALLED "EARTH". OBSERVE THE STRANGE, ALIEN LANDSCAPE. EARTHLINGS CALL THE GREEN BLOBS YOU CAN SEE ON THE MAP "RAINFORESTS". TO FIND OUT MORE ABOUT THEM, OPEN YOUR EARTH FILE DATA BANK FOR THE LATEST INTERPLANETARY REPORT...

WHO?

Interplanetary report number BLOB delta 5.1
Star date: 170361

○ ○ ○

Mission: To observe Planet Earth. (Earthlings call this activity "geography".)

Destination: The bloomin' rainforest

Background: Tests reveal that rainforests are hot, wet and humid (that's Earth-speak for stickily warm). They're packed with tall, woody life-forms called "trees". The forests cover just 6 per cent of the land on Earth but they are inhabited by half of all Earth plants and animals. Watch this space. Further observations will be made.

Report conclusion: In their Earth schools, juvenile Earthlings are informed about rainforests by adult Earthlings called "geography teachers". Meanwhile, Earthlings are chopping the rainforests down for farms and roads.

WARNING! *This is not logical.*

(Obviously geography lessons are just as boring on Planet Blob as they are on Planet Earth!)

Still, rainforests are what this book is all about. Wet enough to soak you to the skin, hot and sticky even in the middle of winter, and home to more creepy-crawlies than ANYWHERE ELSE ON EARTH, rainforests will soon start to grow on you. In *Bloomin' Rainforests*, you can...

- have dinner with the dinosaurs who lived in the first ever rainforests.
- find out why some weird forest fungi glow in the dark.

- learn how to hunt wild animals with the local rainforest people.
- sniff out flowers that stink of smelly socks with top botanist*, Fern. Phwoar!

(*That's the posh name for a horrible scientist who studies plants.)

This is geography like never before. And it's tree-mendously exciting. But if you're thinking of "branching" out on your own, keep your wits about you. Rainforests aren't all about pretty flowers and tropical fruit trees. They can be horribly wild and dangerous. You'll need eyes in the back of your head as you watch out for jaguars on the look-out for lunch, butterflies as big as birds, spiders the size of school dinner-plates and bizarre meat-eating plants.

Whatever you do, stick close to the path – it's easy to get lost. Dead easy. And it can happen to anyone. Even the experts sometimes get it horribly wrong. Which is exactly what happened to intrepid explorer, Percy Fawcett. One fine day, he set off to explore the South American rainforest … and was never seen again. You can read his terrible true story overleaf.

LOST IN THE JUNGLE

London, England, 1906

The dashing young officer with the bushy moustache knocked smartly on the old oak door.

"Come in," boomed a clipped, gruff voice. The officer opened the door and peeked inside the gloomy room. Behind a large desk piled high with dusty maps and books, sat a stern-looking man.

"Ah, Fawcett, good to see you, old chap," he said. "I've got a little job for you. Ever been to Bolivia, dear boy?"

The man was the President of the Royal Geographical Society of Great Britain, an association which mapped and sent explorers to every corner of the globe. His visitor that day was army colonel and all-round good egg, Percy H Fawcett. The President lost no time in explaining what he wanted Fawcett to do. It went something like this...

The Bolivian government wanted some brand-new maps made of their country and they'd asked the Royal Geographical Society for help. And this was where good old Percy came in. Apart from being brave, strong and as tough as old boots, Percy was also a crack cartographer (that's the posh name for a horrible geographer who draws up maps). Just the man for the Bolivian job.

There was just one teeny problem. To make his maps at all accurate, he was going to have to travel through some horribly perilous places. Places where no outsiders had ever been before. Places where the locals didn't take kindly to strangers. Even if Percy survived all that, he might be struck down by a deadly disease or eaten alive by a peckish jaguar. Either way, he'd be a goner. This was no job for a feeble or faint-hearted person!

But plucky Percy wasn't feeble or faint-hearted. Far from it. And he didn't need to be asked twice. In fact, he jumped at the chance to have the adventure of a lifetime. Born by the seaside in Devon, England, in 1867, adventure was Percy's middle name. (His real middle name was Harrison but you get the point.) From an early age, Percy wanted to see the world. Sadly, until he was nineteen years old, all he saw was dull old Devon. Then he joined the British army and was sent off to Sri Lanka, Ireland and Malta. But Percy soon got fed up with army life. It was just too bloomin' boring. Real-life adventure was what he was after. And that's exactly what he got.

South America, 1906–1914

In June 1906, Percy arrived in La Paz, Bolivia, ready to embark on his great adventure. First stop was lofty Lake Titicaca, high up in the peaky Andes Mountains. Getting to the lake was a very rocky road. The thin mountain air made breathing difficult and the mules kept losing their footing on the steep mountain slopes. But did Percy lose heart? Nope, he didn't. Our gutsy hero simply gritted his teeth and plodded grimly on. It would take more than a slippery slope to trip him up. Next, he charted the sources of several raging rivers that poured into the awesome Amazon, and still had time to explore the mighty Mato Grosso (part of the Amazon rainforest in neighbouring Brazil).

If hiking up mountains wasn't tough enough, hacking through the Mato Grosso rainforest really tested his mettle. The flies, the heat, the constant damp really took their toll on Percy and his companions. Before very long, their clothes were soaked through. Then they began to turn mouldy. Day after day, the men chopped their way through a green tangle of vines as thick as human legs and strangling, snake-like creepers. Around every corner danger lurked.

Take gigantic snakes, for starters. One day, Percy and his local guides were paddling gently down river. Imagine the scene. It was a warm, sunny day and life was grand. Percy may well have been whistling. But the peace and quiet didn't last long. Suddenly their flimsy canoe was almost flipped over by ... a truly enormous snake. Its great, ugly head reared out of the water, along with several metres of massive coils.

Unluckily for Percy, he was being attacked by a giant anaconda. The biggest snake in the world. Anacondas can grow up to 10 metres long and measure a metre around the middle. They can catch prey as big as deer and goats, and have terrible table manners. First they grab their victims in their colossal coils and squeeze them to death.

Then they swallow their supper whole. Nasty, very nasty. Was our Percy petrified? Was he, heck. Quick as a flash, he grabbed his gun and shot the revolting reptile stone dead.

And that wasn't all. Another time, Percy and his party were fired on by unfriendly locals. (They only stopped when Percy got out his accordion and started to sing. It must have scared them to death!)

They were harassed by hideous, hairy spiders, bitten half to death by vicious vampire bats and charged at by a bunch of wild bulls. One man even had his fingers chomped off by piranha fish as he was washing his hands in the river! But wild animals weren't their only worry. Their canoe capsized again in the raging rapids and they were nearly washed away by a waterfall.

And later, they almost starved to death when they ran out of food. For ten long days, they lived on nothing but rancid honey and the odd bird's egg until, more bloomin' dead than alive, they managed to kill a deer. The ravenous men ate every bit of it, right down to its fur. (Bet that got stuck in their teeth.)

Finally, in 1914, his map-making done, Percy returned to England. But there was no time for our horrible hero to rest. He was soon off fighting in World War One. When the war ended, Percy was awarded a top medal for bravery but his army days were over. Despite his brush with starvation and the weird wildlife, he was itching to get back to the rainforest again.

The Amazon rainforest, Brazil, 1925
At last, in spring 1925, Percy set off for Brazil again. He'd been back to the jungle several times in between to get to know the region better. But this time muddlesome maps were the last thing on his mind. You see, for years, Percy had dreamed of a fabulous city with beautiful buildings made from silver and gold, and gorgeous statues made from glittering crystal. He'd read about the city, which he curiously called "Z", in an ancient library book. Now he wanted to see it with his own eyes.

The only snag was that the city was thought to lie right in the middle of the deepest, darkest jungle. Where no outsider had ever set foot before. Did Percy find his long-lost city? Or did he perish in the attempt? Here's how the newspapers of the time might have reported what happened next…

INTREPID EXPLORER STILL MISSING

Concern is growing for plucky British explorer, Colonel Percy H Fawcett, feared lost in the jungle. Fawcett, 58, was last seen in person in April when he and his eldest son, John, set off into the jungle with a family friend, Raleigh Rimell. Their goal was to find a fabulous, long-lost city of gold which Fawcett believed lay in the heart of the rainforest.

FAWCETT & SON

In May, the men said goodbye to their local guides and their faithful packhorses. The tangled terrain made riding difficult so they chose to carry on on foot, alone, carrying their own baggage.

BACK-PACKING

The guides brought back a note from Fawcett for his wife, addressed eerily "Dead Horse Camp". It read, "You need have no fear of any failure." Nothing has been heard from him since.

Despite Fawcett's instructions to his friends that they should not risk their lives trying to rescue him, there are plans to send out a search team soon.

ON THE LOOK OUT

when it comes to exploring. In fact, he's as hard as nails. Besides, he's brilliant at reading maps and he's never, ever got lost before. If anyone can make it out alive, it's our Percy." We hope he is right.

One close friend told our reporter, "Percy's a real pro

Sadly, this was to be Percy's last jungle journey. Search party after search party set out for the forest but no trace of Percy was ever found. Not long afterwards the rumours began. It was difficult to know what to believe. Had Percy been eaten by alligators? Or had he caught a fatal fever and died? Was he hopelessly lost?

HOLD ON! I THINK WE TURN LEFT HERE

Or had he in fact found his city and was he now living there happily ever after? Truth is, nobody knew.

Some years later, one man claimed to have got to the bottom of the mystery, once and for all. He said Percy had been killed by hostile locals and, what's more, he'd got Percy's bones to prove it. Could he be telling the tragic

172

truth? Well, the funny bones were taken off to England and examined by bone experts. But guess what? They turned out to belong to somebody else, after all. So what actually happened to poor lost Percy Fawcett? To this day, nobody really knows.

So, as you can see, rainforests can be horribly dangerous but they're also bloomin' brilliant and fascinating as well. So what on Earth are these perilous places and where can you find one, if you dare? Is it *really* like a jungle out there? Or is their "bark" worse than their bite? You'll find the answers to all of these questions as you "leaf" through this book...

HOT AND STICKY

The best way to find out what a rainforest is like is to go and see one for yourself. But if there isn't a rainforest near where you live, what on Earth can you do? Well, why not try this simple experiment? (Unless you *want* to go without pocket money for the rest of your life, ask permission first.)

Go into your bedroom and turn the heating on full.

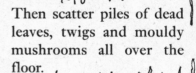

Then scatter piles of dead leaves, twigs and mouldy mushrooms all over the floor.

Grab some pot plants (rubber plants work well) and stand them on the ground. (You'll need to pick some good, tall ones for the towering rainforest trees.)

If you're feeling really brave, release a handful of spiders and some creepy-crawlies into the room. They'll give the place a nice, lived-in look.

Now get a watering can and give the whole thing a good soaking. This will make your room horribly hot and steamy. Just like a real rainforest.

(OK, so it might be better to use your imagination for this last bit.)

First rainforests

The first rainforests grew about 150 million years ago. (Even your teacher isn't that bloomin' old.) These ancient forests were packed with giant conifer trees that dinosaurs once munched. Incredibly, some of these prehistoric plants still grow today. Take maddening monkey-puzzle trees, for example. (You might have seen them growing in gardens.) They got their name because muddled monkeys couldn't puzzle out how to climb up their spiky branches.

There were even bloomin' rainforests in Britain. Don't believe me? Well, it's true. British botanists have found fossil pollen grains from ancient rainforest trees that bloomed about 50 million years ago. (The weather was much warmer then.)

Earth-shattering fact

The name rainforest was coined in the nineteenth century by German geographer and botanist, Alfred Schimper. He thought it fitted because the forests were so bloomin' wet. (OK, so you didn't need to be a brain surgeon to work that out.) Some people call them jungles instead. "Jungle" actually comes from an old Indian word which actually means, er, desert or wasteland! Confusing, or what? Later the word changed to mean a thick tangle of tropical plants and trees. In other words, a bloomin' rainforest.

Where on Earth do bloomin' rainforests grow?

Hi, Fern here. Being a botanist, I'm mad about plants so rainforests are right up my street. So where can you find one if you need one? Well, rainforests cover about six per cent of the Earth – that's about the size of the USA. They grow in three enormous chunks in South America, Africa and South-East Asia with bits and pieces on the Pacific Islands. Down under, Australians also claim to have some in Queensland. So you've probably got quite a long way to go. Here's a handy map to show you where on Earth you can root a rainforest out.

NORTH AMERICA

ATLANTIC OCEAN

ASIA

PAPUA NEW GUINEA

INDIA

AFRICA

COLUMBIA

VENUZUELA

PACIFIC OCEAN

BURMA

ZAIRE

INDIAN OCEAN

BRAZIL

PERU

SOUTH AMERICA

INDONESIA

BOLIVIA

AUSTRALIA

ANTARCTICA

Could you recognize a rainforest?

If you ask a geographer to describe a rainforest, don't worry
if he or she starts spouting ancient history...

> *Never have I beheld so fair a thing;*
> *trees beautiful and green, with flowers*
> *and fruits each according to their kind;*
> *many birds, and little birds which sing*
> *very sweetly.*

Yuk! Slushy, or what? Actually it was ace explorer,
Christopher Columbus, who wrote this in 1492 in a letter to
the King and Queen of Spain. But it's no good going all
gooey-eyed. In nature, things aren't always quite as pretty
and sweet as they first seem. If you want to be a budding
geographer, you'll have to do better than that. Wouldn't
know a rainforest if it grew in your own back garden? Don't
worry. Help is at hand. But first, here's Fern with the
rainforest weather forecast...

> Today will start off hot and sticky with clear
> skies in the morning. It'll cloud
> over in the afternoon and
> there's a good chance of a
> thunderstorm with torrential
> rain. Don't bother with a
> brolly – you'll still get
> soaking wet. Tomorrow will
> be much the same, and the
> next day, and the next day,
> and the day after that...

Anyway, there are three easy ways of recognizing a rainforest by its weird weather. Generally speaking, rainforests are:

Steaming hot
It's always hot in the rainforest, whatever time of the year you go. So if you're hoping for a white Christmas, you're in for a very long wait. In the bloomin' rainforest, it's summer all year long. Temperatures can reach a baking 30°C by day and it's not much cooler at night. And every day's the same. So why are rainforests so horribly hot? Well, it's to do with where on Earth they grow. Rainforests bloom in the steamy tropics along the equator. (That's an imaginary line around the Earth. It splits the Earth into north and south.) Here the sun always shines straight overhead so its warming rays are seriously strong.

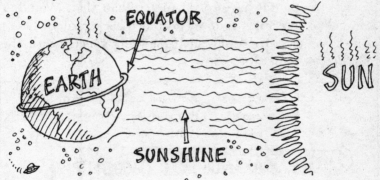

Soaking wet
If you're heading for the rainforest, expect to get wet through. It pours with rain almost every day. Horrible geographers count rainforests as places which get at least 2,000 millimetres of rain a year. Wet, or what? The reason rainforests are so bloomin' wet is because they're so close to the equator. Here's what happens:

179

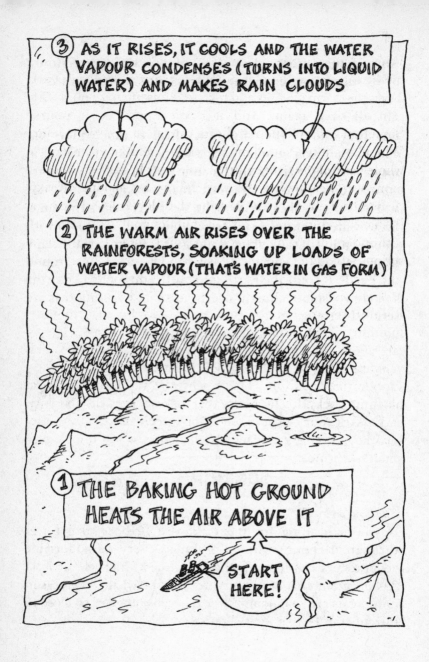

What's more, because it's so wet and hot, the rain that falls on the forest trees quickly evaporates (turns into water gas). Then the warm air rises and forms clouds, then it pours with rain all over again. And it never rains but it pours. Sometimes 60 millimetres of rain can fall in one single hour. Which might not sound much, but it would be like having a whole bathful of water emptied over your head! And there's more wet weather on the way. In the afternoon, the sky turns purply black with towering thunderclouds. There's a flash of lightning and a crash of thunder and – hey presto! – a thunderstorm's on its way. Watch out, you're in for a serious soaking.

Horribly humid

Rainforests are horribly hot and sticky because of high humidity. That's the tricky technical term scientists use to talk about the amount of water vapour in the air. (Water vapour's water in gas form.) Warm air can hold more water vapour than cold air. That's why the rainforest feels so bloomin' sticky. It's humidity that makes you sweat like a pig and makes your clothes go horribly green and mouldy. You see, they never get a chance to dry out. So you'll look and smell *really* nice!

If all this has left you too worn out to drag yourself outside at break, try this scientific-sounding excuse. Put up your hand and say politely:

Your teacher will be so flummoxed you might get away with it. But what on Earth is wrong with you?

Answer: Oh dear, going outside's the best thing for you, I'm afraid. How unlucky is that? You see, hygrophilous (high-gro-filus) is the posh word for a plant that grows outside where it's nice and humid and damp. Somewhere just like a bloomin' rainforest. And no, it isn't catching. But be careful *you* don't catch a cold!

Earth-shattering fact

If you set out to walk from one end of the Amazon rainforest to the other, it would take you at least a month. Even if you walked all night and day. You see, the Amazon's the biggest rainforest on Earth, by a very long chalk. It blooms along the banks of the awesome Amazon River in South America and covers an enormous six million square kilometres. That's almost as big as Australia. By rainforest standards, that's bloomin' huge.

Spotter's guide to rainforests

You might think all rainforests look the same but you get lots of different types. Trouble is it's tricky telling them apart because they've got so many things in common. For a start, all rainforests are hot and wet. They're all lush and green and steamy. And they're all bursting with amazing animals and plants. So how on Earth can you tell them apart? Well, it all depends where they grow. Still can't see the wood for the trees? Why not check out Fern's quick rainforest factfile and find your way out of the tangle?

1

Name: LOWLAND RAINFORESTS

Location: Low-lying land around the equator

Forest features: These fabulous forests are hot and wet and packed with tall, evergreen trees (they're trees that stay green all year round). Some of these bloomers grow more than 45 metres tall and some, called "emergents" (they pop out of the top), can reach 90 metres. Their tops form a thick, leafy roof over the forest which botanists like me call the canopy. Lowland forests are teeming with plants and animals. Awesome, isn't it?

You'll get to know these forests better because they're what this book is mostly about.

2

Name: MONTANE FORESTS

Location: High up on tropical mountains or hills

Forest features: These hillside forests are cooler than those that grow lower down. And the higher you go, the colder it gets. They're dank, damp and covered in clinging cloud. (That's why they're also called cloud forests.)

They're the perfect place for hygrophilous (remember they're plants that like the heat and damp) bloomers such as mosses, lichens and ferns. They sprout in the gloomy undergrowth.

3
Name: MANGROVE FORESTS
Location: Along tropical coasts
Forest features: These are huge, muddy swamps where tropical
rivers flow into the sea. They're named after mangrove trees.
These unusual bloomers have long, tangled roots for gripping
the mud as the tide tries to shift it. They've also got roots
that stick out of the water like titchy snorkels for sucking in
oxygen so the trees can breathe. Brilliant, isn't it?

Freaky fish skip about on the mud. You could say they're fish
out of water, ha, ha! In fact, they're called mudskippers (howls
of amazement!). The biggest mangrove forest stretches for
260 kilometres along the Bay of Bengal, between India and
Bangladesh. But if you're planning a paddle, watch out for
tigers – they love to gobble up fishermen.

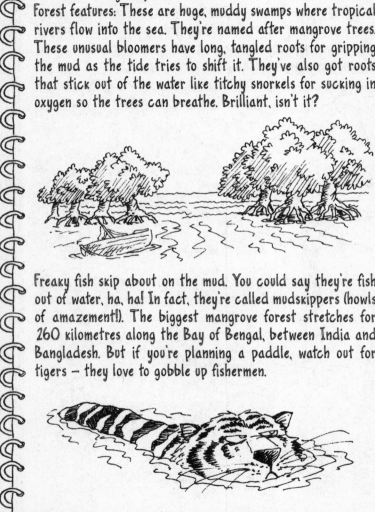

4

Name: FLOODED FORESTS

Location: Along the banks of tropical rivers

Forest features: When a river bursts its banks, it floods the forest around it. The forest can stay underwater for months on end. The water rises by some 15 metres, drowning all but the tallest trees. It's tough luck on the birds and monkeys that live among the branches. They're left high and dry when their homes get flooded out. But it's great news for hungry forest fish. They swim among the underwater tree trunks, guzzling fruit and seeds.

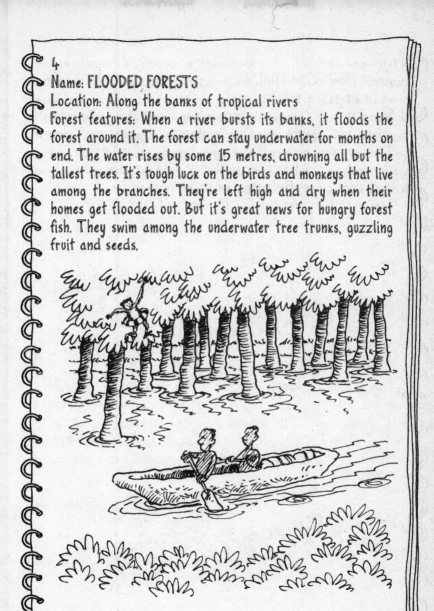

That's all very well, you might say, but aren't forests horribly boring? I mean, what do trees actually do, apart from stand around all day? It's not like you can take a tree for a nice, long walk, is it? You'd be better off getting a dog. But you couldn't be more wrong. The bloomin' rainforests are bursting with some horribly exciting and interesting plants. And guess what? Yep. There *is* even a tree that likes to go for walks. Read on if you don't believe me.

ᚱAINFOREST ᛒLOOMERS

The first thing you'll notice about the rainforest is all the bloomin' greenery. (Well, what did you expect?) It's like being inside a huge greenhouse, and I mean HUGE. The steamy rainforest heat's perfect for plants to grow all year round. And all that rain means they get loads of water to slurp. But you won't find boring tomatoes and prize dahlias growing in here. Not like the ones your grandad grows in his greenhouse. Oh no. Rainforest fruit and veg is far freakier than that. You'll find trees as tall as 20 geography teachers, flowers that reek of mouldy old cheese, and vicious vines that strangle their neighbours. Eek! Is that weird enough for you? Are you brave enough to sneak a closer look? Here's Fern to show you around.

A rainforest: the inside story

Well, here I am in the bloomin' rainforest, surrounded by fabulous foliage. It's heavenly! Anyway, before I get carried away, there are a few things you should know. The first is that rainforest trees grow in layers, depending how tall they are. Our tour starts right at the very top. What d'ya mean, you're not coming with me?

189

LAYER 1: EMERGENTS

I'M NOT TOO GOOD WITH HEIGHTS SO YOU'LL HAVE TO FORGIVE ME IF I GET A BIT... OOH! BEST NOT TO LOOK DOWN. I'M HERE AMONG THE TALLEST TREES IN THE FOREST AND WHEN I SAY TALL, I MEAN TALL. THEIR TOPS POKE OUT AT A SCARY 60m ABOVE THE GROUND. EACH TREETOP'S THE SIZE OF A SOCCER PITCH. SO WE'RE TALKING PRETTY BIG BLOOMERS HERE. BECAUSE THEY'RE SO TALL, THEY TAKE A BIT OF A BATTERING FROM THE HOWLING WINDS AND START TO SWAY. HELP! THEY ALSO GET STRUCK BY LIGHTNING. AND THEY'RE HOME TO MASSIVE MONKEY-EATING EAGLES. LET'S HOPE THEY DON'T EAT GEOGRAPHERS! JUST IN CASE, I'M OUTTA HERE!

LAYER 2: CANOPY

PHEW! THAT'S BETTER. KIND OF. THE THINGS I DO IN THE NAME OF GEOGRAPHY. THE CANOPY'S LIKE A HUGE, GREEN UMBRELLA OVER THE FOREST. HERE, THE TREETOPS MAKE A LUSCIOUS LAYER OF JUICY LEAVES ABOUT 6m THICK, AND IT'S NICE AND WARM, THOUGH I'M ALREADY SOAKING WET. BUT THESE CONDITIONS MAKE A PERFECT HOME FOR THE RAINFOREST'S OTHER INHABITANTS, AND TWO THIRDS OF ALL THE FOREST PLANTS AND ANIMALS LIVE HERE IN THE CANOPY. SO IT'S A BIT CROWDED UP HERE, TO SAY THE LEAST. I THINK I MIGHT MOVE ON DOWN AND GET A BIT NEARER TO THE GROUND

LAYER 3: UNDERSTOREY

SMALL TREES, LIKE SPINDLY PALMS AND SAPLINGS, SPROUT DOWN HERE. NOT EXACTLY STRONG ENOUGH TO HOLD UP A GEOGRAPHER LIKE ME, SO I WON'T HANG AROUND. THEY GROW BEST IN GAPS LEFT WHEN OLD TREES DIE OR A STORM BLOWS THEM OVER. THAT GIVES THE SAPLINGS A CHANCE TO GRAB SOME OF THE SUNLIGHT. THE TREES HERE GROW ABOUT 15m HIGH AND THEY'RE COVERED IN TANGLED VINES AND CREEPERS. TARZAN WOULD HAVE FELT RIGHT AT HOME. NOW WHERE'S THAT BLOOMIN' ROPE GONE? AAARGHHHH!

LAYER 4 : FOREST FLOOR

AHEM, BIT OF A BUMPY LANDING THERE BUT NOTHING BROKEN, THANK GOODNESS. DOWN HERE, IT'S SO BLOOMIN' DARK AND GLOOMY NOTHING MUCH CAN GROW APART FROM MASSES OF DAMP-LOVING MOSSES, FUNGI* AND FERNS. (BRILLIANT FOR BREAKING FALLS.) THE GROUND'S LITTERED WITH OLD, DEAD LEAVES WHERE MILLIPEDES AND OTHER CREEPY-CRAWLIES LURK. (DID I TELL YOU I'M SCARED OF INSECTS? WELL I AM...) AND WATCH YOUR STEP. THAT BIT OF WOOD MIGHT LOOK LIKE A HARMLESS BRANCH BUT IT COULD BE A DEADLY POISONOUS SNAKE. HISSSSS!

* THAT'S WHAT BOTANISTS LIKE ME CALL THINGS LIKE MUSHROOMS, MOULDS AND TOADSTOOLS

Horrible Health Warning

You take your socks off after a hard day's hike, and shock horror! Your toes have gone all mouldy and green! Don't panic. In the steamy rainforest, things go off very fast. The gruesome green mould's actually a type of fungus that normally scoffs dead leaves and animal bodies from the forest floor. But they'll eat smelly feet too – lucky they're not fussy. The greedy fungi guzzle valuable chemicals from their food. Then, when they die and rot, the chemicals go into the soil. Which is great news for rainforest trees. Their roots suck the nourishing chemicals up and use them to grow. To cure your pongy problem, you need to let your feet dry out. Easier said than done.

Eight tree-mendous plant facts

Could you be a budding botanist like Fern? Turn your teacher green with envy with these tree-mendous plant facts. But be warned. Rainforest plants don't sprout in nice, neat, well-behaved rows like the roses and daffs in your dad's flower beds. These bloomers are green, mean and dangerous to know, and they grow like mad all over the place…

1 How many trees grow in a rainforest? Millions is the answer. It would take you years to count them all. Are you *really* that desperate to miss double geography? But you'd have trouble finding two trees the same. In a patch of rainforest the size of a soccer pitch, there may be 200 different types of tree. It might not sound much but in temperate forests (they grow in colder parts of the world), you'd be lucky to find ten.

2 Think of your house, with another nine houses balanced on top. That's how bloomin' high the tallest rainforest trees grow. To stop them toppling over in the wind, massive roots grow from their trunks and anchor the tree in the ground. The roots are a bit like the guy ropes that hold up a tent. Except that they can be an amazing 5 metres high – think how big that would make your tent!

3 Some plants can't reach the sun on their own. They have to hitch a lift on another plant. For instance, lianas are woody, jungle vines, as thick as a person's leg. They can grow 200 metres long and are strong enough to swing on. (Remember all those old Tarzan films?) A young liana grows roots in the ground, just like a normal plant. Then it winds itself round a nearby tree. As the tree grows, the liana grows with it up towards the sun. Simple as that.

4 Rainforest trees have to grow tall to reach the sun. But it's not because they want a suntan. You see, plants can't just pop along to the shops if they're feeling peckish. They have to make their own fast food and they need the sun to do it. Here's what they do...

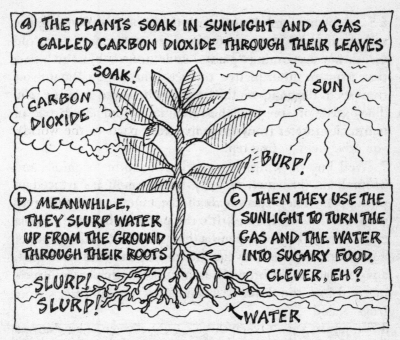

5 When a tree crashes down in the forest, it's bad news for forest floor plants. They get squashed flat. But that doesn't stop the amazing stilt palm. This ingenious bloomer sprouts stilt-like roots and walks away from the tangle. Yes, this is one plant you really *can* take for a walk.

6 Some plants don't bother with the ground at all. Botanists call them epiphytes (epi-fites). This comes from two old Greek words meaning "plants" and "upon". They're plants that grow on other plants, you see. These high-fliers grow from seeds blown up on the breeze or dropped in birds' poo. They settle on tree branches, then their roots dangle down and suck in water from the moist air.

7 Well-known epiphytes include exotic orchids and bromeliads (bro-mell-ee-ads). Bromeliads are related to pineapples. Their spiky leaves form a bucket which fills up with water when it rains. It's the perfect place for a forest frog nursery! What happens is this. The mother frog lays her eggs near by. When they hatch into tadpoles, she gives them a piggy-back to the bromeliad pond. The tadpoles eat insects that fall into the water and soon grow up into big, strong frogs. Aaah!

YIPEEE!

HOP OFF!

8 Competition for sunlight can be fierce in the forest. So some plants have dirty tricks up their leaves, sorry, sleeves. Take the sinister strangler fig, for example. This vile vegetable sprouts high up on a tree branch, then wraps itself around the trunk, tighter and tighter… Meanwhile, its roots dig into the ground and steal the tree's supply of water.

Slowly the foul fig strangles the tree and blocks out all its light. The tree dies and rots away, leaving a terrible trellis of fig roots behind.

Designer bloomers

No, they're *not* those giant knickers grannies often wear. You know the ones I mean! These bloomers are rainforest flowers. Not all rainforest flowers are sneaky and mean like the frightful strangler fig. In fact, some are sickeningly pretty and sweet. But their fabulous features aren't just for show. They're for impressing birds and other creatures for pollination*.

*Pollination is how flowers make their seeds. Flowers are filled with yellow dust called pollen. To pollinate, the pollen needs to shift to another flower of the same type of plant. Most rainforest flowers use animals to carry their pollen from one plant to another. Then the plant makes seeds that grow into baby plants. So, you see, pollination's pretty vital. Without it there wouldn't be any bloomin' rainforests at all. That's why flowers go to so much bother.

197

But first they need to grab the animal's attention. And for this they need to look GOOD. That means perfume, colour and designer flowers. Yes, the whole bloomin' works. What's in it for the animals, you might ask? Well, they get to nosh on tasty nectar – that's a sweet, sticky syrup flowers make.

But animals don't just find any old flower to visit. They're much pickier than that. Many flowers are exclusively designed for one particular type of creature. So, if you were a hungry hummingbird, which of these three designer bloomers would you head for?

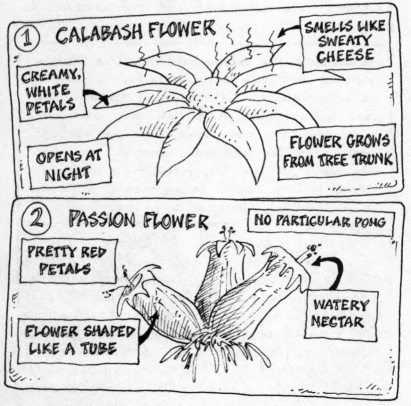

1. CALABASH FLOWER

SMELLS LIKE SWEATY CHEESE

CREAMY, WHITE PETALS

OPENS AT NIGHT

FLOWER GROWS FROM TREE TRUNK

2. PASSION FLOWER

NO PARTICULAR PONG

PRETTY RED PETALS

FLOWER SHAPED LIKE A TUBE

WATERY NECTAR

③ BUCKET ORCHID

LOVELY SMELL

BRIGHT YELLOW FLOWER WITH BIG RED SPOTS

BUCKET SHAPED FLOWER

TWO WING SHAPED PETALS

Answer:

2 These two are made for each other. Birds have excellent eyesight and like bright colours but they can't smell a thing. So there's no point in the flowers they visit having a strong pong. The hummingbird's long beak is brilliant for poking about deep inside flowers, before it slurps up the nectar with its long tongue. As it does this, pollen sticks on to its head.

By the way, hummingbirds may be tiny (some are only as big as bees!) but they've got truly gigantic appetites. To keep up, you'd need to scoff about 130 loaves of bread a day – that's more than 1,000 rounds of cheese sandwiches. Burp!

In case you were wondering, the perfect pollinator for **1** is a bat. Bats are nocturnal (that means they fly about at night and doze during the day) and that's when this clever flower blooms. It's white so it's easy to see in the dark. Bats love flowers with a cheesy pong because they smell just like the bats do. And it's easy for bats to reach the flowers because they grow straight out of the tree trunk. That way, the bats don't snag their delicate wings on the sharp branches and there's plenty of room to manoeuvre.

Flower 3 is pollinated by bees. They think it smells just heavenly. Its petals act like spotty signposts to guide the bees in to land. A bee tries to perch on the edge of the bucket but it's horribly slimy and slippery. The bewildered bee loses its footing and tumbles in with a splash! The bucket's full of water. Is there any escape? Yes, but it isn't easy. The bewildered bee has to force its way up a narrow tunnel inside the flower and out of a side door. But not before two big blobs of pollen have landed on his back. Splat!

Say it with flowers

Have you noticed how flowers do strange things to people? How they make even geography teachers go all gooey-eyed? Desperate to get into *your* teacher's good books? Why not say it with a big bunch of rainforest flowers? Only NOT these freaky blooms. They're definitely not to be sniffed at. To find out how *not* to get up your teacher's nose, pop into Auntie Fleur's Freaky Flower Shop.

Welcome to Auntie Fleur's Freaky Flower Shop, petals. You'll find flowers for every occasion in here. Even quite smelly and unpleasant ones. Here are four of my own particular favourites...

NAME: RAFFLESIA
WHERE IT GROWS: BORNEO, SUMATRA, INDONESIA

APPEARANCE: GIANT ORANGE-BROWN BLOOM SHAPED LIKE A SCHOOL CABBAGE. LEATHERY PETALS COVERED IN WARTS. IT'S THE WORLD'S BIGGEST FLOWER, GROWING UP TO A METRE ACROSS.

THE BLOOMIN' DETAILS:

① IT GROWS INSIDE THE ROOTS OF RAINFOREST VINES AND SUCKS OUT THEIR LIFE JUICES.

② IT'S ALSO KNOWN AS THE "STINKING CORPSE LILY" BECAUSE IT REEKS OF ROTTING FLESH. PHWOAR!

③ ITS PUTRID PONG ATTRACTS FLIES FOR POLLINATION. THEY THINK IT'S A TASTY MEAL. OH DEAR.

If you want to say it with flowers, I'd stick to roses, if I were you. Unless you're buying it for someone you really don't like. I mean, it's not like they'll ever talk to you again.

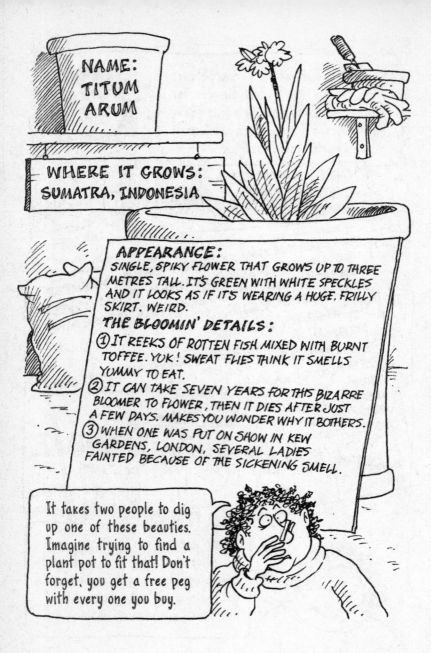

NAME:
TITUM
ARUM

WHERE IT GROWS:
SUMATRA, INDONESIA

APPEARANCE:
SINGLE, SPIKY FLOWER THAT GROWS UP TO THREE METRES TALL. IT'S GREEN WITH WHITE SPECKLES AND IT LOOKS AS IF IT'S WEARING A HUGE, FRILLY SKIRT. WEIRD.

THE BLOOMIN' DETAILS:

① IT REEKS OF ROTTEN FISH MIXED WITH BURNT TOFFEE. YUK! SWEAT FLIES THINK IT SMELLS YUMMY TO EAT.

② IT CAN TAKE SEVEN YEARS FOR THIS BIZARRE BLOOMER TO FLOWER, THEN IT DIES AFTER JUST A FEW DAYS. MAKES YOU WONDER WHY IT BOTHERS.

③ WHEN ONE WAS PUT ON SHOW IN KEW GARDENS, LONDON, SEVERAL LADIES FAINTED BECAUSE OF THE SICKENING SMELL.

It takes two people to dig up one of these beauties. Imagine trying to find a plant pot to fit that! Don't forget, you get a free peg with every one you buy.

202

NAME:
TROPICAL
STINKHORN FUNGUS

WHERE IT GROWS:
SOUTH AMERICA

APPEARANCE:
LONG, SLIMY SPIKE COVERED IN WHITE, LACY VEIL.

THE BLOOMIN' DETAILS:

1. THIS FREAKY FUNGUS REALLY LIVES UP TO ITS NAME. IT REEKS OF ROTTEN MEAT AND SMELLY TOILETS.
2. FOREST FLIES FLOCK TO THE FUNGUS TO GUZZLE ON THE DISGUSTING SLIME. MEANWHILE, THEIR BODIES GET DUSTED WITH SPORES (TINY SPECKS THAT FUNGI GROW FROM).
3. SOME RAINFOREST FUNGI GLOW IN THE DARK. EVEN THE EXPERTS DON'T KNOW WHY. IT MIGHT BE FOR SCARING OFF HUNGRY BEETLES THAT LIKE TO NIBBLE THE FUNGI AT NIGHT.

This bloomer's really lovely to look at. An excellent choice for birthdays and Christmas. If you want your house to smell like a cesspit and swarm with flies, that is.

NAME: PITCHER PLANT
WHERE IT GROWS: AFRICA, SOUTH EAST ASIA, SOUTH AMERICA, AUSTRALIA

THE BLOOMIN' DETAILS:

1. AN INSECT LANDS ON THE RIM OF THE PITCHER, LOOKING FOR YUMMY NECTAR TO DRINK. BUT IT'S IN FOR A NASTY SHOCK. IT SLIPS ON THE WAXY SURFACE AND PLUNGES INTO A POOL OF WATER INSIDE. THERE'S NO ESCAPE. THE PLANT SQUIRTS OUT DIGESTIVE JUICES TO DISSOLVE ITS BODY. THEN IT SOAKS ITS VICTIM UP.

2. SOME PITCHER PLANTS LOOK LIKE TRUMPETS, CHAMPAGNE GLASSES AND LANTERNS. THERE'S EVEN ONE SHAPED LIKE A TOILET. COMPLETE WITH TOILET LID!

3. THE BIGGEST PITCHER PLANT IS THE RAJAH PITCHER. ITS FOUL FLOWER CAN HOLD A BUCKETFUL OF WATER AND TRAP VICTIMS AS BIG AS MICE.

Well, they say pride comes before a fall. But if pitchers are your cup of tea, and there's no accounting for taste, don't forget you'll need a good supply of fresh flies to feed your fiendish flower with.

Earth-shattering fact

Durian fruit reek of rotten fish but they taste delicious. Especially to orangutans. These awesome apes love slurping the yummy custard-like flesh inside. They're too busy stuffing their faces to spit out the seeds. Later they have a poo and the seeds plop out. (Better not mention these disgusting details while you're having tea with your squeamish old aunt.)

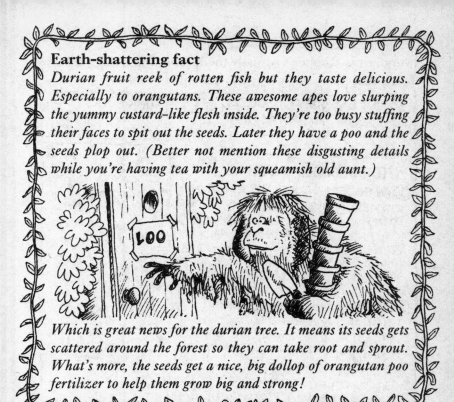

Which is great news for the durian tree. It means its seeds gets scattered around the forest so they can take root and sprout. What's more, the seeds get a nice, big dollop of orangutan poo fertilizer to help them grow big and strong!

Scandalous seeds

You might think flower seeds are pretty harmless and spend their lives quietly growing into new plants. You probably wouldn't expect a humble handful of seeds to cause a shocking scandal. But believe it or not, they did. The seeds in question were rubber-tree seeds. Read on and discover the whole shocking story.

A rubbery discovery

Rubber trees grow in the South American rainforest. Their posh scientific name is *Hevea brasiliensis*, in case you were wondering. Rubber's actually made from the milky juice, or latex, that oozes out when you cut slits in their bark.

And it's horribly useful. You can turn it into loads of useful things, like car tyres and rubber bands. And you can use it to rub out mistakes when you're doing your geography homework. What's more, it's cheap and easy to grow. No wonder horrible humans saw rubber as a way to get rich, quick.

The first European to see wild rubber trees was posh French explorer and scientist, Charles Marie de la Condamine (1701–1774). (Of course, local people had known about rubber for years. They used it for making bouncy rubber balls and waterproofing their canoes.)

In 1743, Charles sailed down the Amazon River on a raft and wrote a book about his adventures. Among the things he wrote notes about were getting a painful shock from an electric eel and seeing his first rubber tree. He even made a rubber carrier bag for his things and sent some bits of rubber home as souvenirs.

When news of de la Condamine's discovery reached Europe, it caused a massive stir. You see, apart from being able to bounce, rubber was brilliant for keeping things dry. Scottish scientist, Charles Macintosh, used rubber to make wellington boots and raincoats snug and waterproof. (That's how macintoshes got their name.) Then an American inventor, Charles Goodyear, worked out how to make rubber into tyres for the recently invented car. There was no looking back. Soon rubber was all the rage. Trouble was, it only grew in far-off Brazil where trade was controlled by wealthy businessmen called rubber barons. No doubt they were rubbing their hands with glee.

Young British botanist, Henry Wickham (1845–1928) soon put a stop to all that. In 1876, the government hired him to smuggle some rubber-tree seeds out of Brazil. Henry jumped at the chance. After all, he'd got nothing better to do.

He collected 70,000 rubber seeds and packed them into crates, carefully wrapped in banana leaves. Then he hired a ship to carry his precious cargo back to Britain.

If anyone asked, Henry pretended he needed the seeds for the royal plant collection at London's Kew Gardens. Otherwise, the authorities would never have let him leave with his illegal booty. Luckily for him, they believed his excuse and he and the seeds reached home safely. Back at Kew Gardens, nearly 7,000 of the precious seeds sprouted into tiny rubber trees. These were packed off to Sri Lanka and Malaysia to grow on huge plantations. Within a few years, there were millions of trees, producing millions of tonnes of cheap rubber a year. The Brazilian rubber barons were ruined.

As for Henry, he was paid £700 for his trouble and given a knighthood. But the scandal surrounding the stolen seeds never died away. Some people said he'd done a great service for his country. Others accused him of being a petty plant criminal. Today, this kind of plant pilfering would never be allowed. Fed up with all the fuss, Henry moved to Australia to try his hand at growing tobacco and coffee. But he ended up losing all of his money in a shady deal. Poor Henry never really bounced back. What a bloomin' shame.

But plants aren't the only things lurking in the rainforest undergrowth. Ever get the feeling you're being watched? Well, you are! It's time to meet some seriously shady characters. If you dare...

SHADY CHARACTERS

Picture the scene. It's mid-afternoon in the rainforest. You've got the freakiest feeling you're being watched. But apart from the odd, lonesome lizard, there's no one else around. Weird. A lot of the animals on the planet live in the bloomin' rainforest. So where on Earth are they all? You might not be able to see them but they're there, believe me. The thing is, many of these shady characters are nocturnal. That means they doze all day and come out at dusk for the night shift when they hunt for food. (Other animals are out and about during the day and go to sleep at night. That way, there's always plenty of food to go round.) Others are just plain shy. So you have to use different ways of finding out when an animal's about. But here's an amazing fact. The most common animals in the rainforest aren't big brutes or hairy beasts. They're incredible insects and other ugly bugs.

Scientists who study insects are called entomologists (ent-o-moll-ogists). They get their name from an old Greek word for "cut up". This is because an insect's body looks like it's been "cut up" into three. Guess how entomologists find out about insects? Yep, they chop the insects up. (I expect the insects were pretty "cut up" about that!) Anyway, I'm sticking to flowers. All this talk about insects is giving me the creeps.

Ants in your pants

Lift any mossy old stone in your garden and chances are some creepy-crawly will scurry out. Look in any dark nook or cranny and you're bound to disturb a spider. But guess where you'll find more insects than anywhere else on Planet Earth? Yep, in the bloomin' rainforest. Shake any rainforest tree and a staggering 1,500 different types of insects might come fluttering out. It's true.

Entomologists have counted at least one million types of rainforest insect but there may be millions more out there. Most of them are tiny but they're capable of some outsized feats. Take awesome ants, for starters…

1 How many types of ants live in one rainforest tree? Give up? The answer's about 50. This might not sound very much to you but you'd only find 50 in the *whole* of Britain. Multiply that by millions of rainforest trees, and that's an awful lot of ants. In fact, scientists think ants account for a third of all rainforest creatures. And they get absolutely everywhere from inside plants to inside your pants. Mind you don't get bitten!

2 Leaf-cutter ants are seriously small fry. But they're also immensely strong. These incredible insects can lift 50 times their own body weight in leaves. That would be like a human weight-lifter picking up an elephant. Now that *would* be awesome.

3 Leaf-cutter ants cut up leaves and carry them back to their underground nest. They chew them up and mix the bits with droppings and spit to make a compost heap. Then they grow fungus on it to eat. The house-proud ants keep their gardens neat and tidy and pull out any unwanted weeds.

211

4 Tailor ants make their own cosy tree nests from leaves stitched together with silk. But they don't use needles and thread for sewing. That would be too boring. They use their own ant grubs instead, passing them backwards and forwards between two leaves.

THIS IS GIVING ME A HEADACHE!

Meanwhile, the adult ants give the grubs a gentle squeeze to get the silk flowing from their mouths. Thank goodness your parents don't do this to you!

5 Some plants have their own pet ants living inside their stems and leaves. Azteca ants live inside the trunks of trumpet trees. The ants take a store of tiny insects along and live off sugary juices these insects make. So the ants get a safe place to shelter and plenty to eat. But what's in it for the patient plants? Well, Azteca ants can't sting but they've got a horribly painful bite. Which makes them brilliant bodyguards. Anyone who comes near their tree-house gets well and truly nipped. Then the angry ants squirt acid into the wound just for good measure! Ouch!

6 If you thought these awful ants were appalling, think again. In the jungles of South America lurks an even angrier ant than that. And it'll have you running for your life! Trouble is, this fierce creature doesn't travel alone. It's part of an awesome army, at least 20 million ants strong. This terrifying troop marches through the forest, devouring anything daft enough to get in its way. It strips frogs, snakes and even birds to skeletons. Very creepy! But army ants can be horribly useful, believe it or not. They raid people's homes and gobble up cockroaches and other insect pests. Don't worry, the horrible humans get well out of the way first. Byeee!

OK, STOP TALKING AT THE BACK. READY? QUICK MARCH!

Earth-shattering fact

If big, hairy spiders make you shudder, you might like to skip the next bit. The biggest, hairiest spiders IN THE WORLD live in the Amazon rainforest. They're called bird-eating spiders, and they're HUGE. Including their horrible, hairy legs, each one's the size of a school dinner-plate. Imagine finding one of these whoppers in your sausage and mash! What's worse, they've got terrible table manners. A spider pounces on a passing bird and gives it a deadly poisonous bite. Then it sucks its victim's juices out. Nasty. Very nasty.

MENU BIRD

Mad about beetles – the amazing Amazon adventures of Wallace and Bates

Creepy-crawlies do strange things to people. Some people can't even spy a spider without shrieking with fear. Other people find them fascinating. Yes, it takes all sorts. Take beetle-mad British scientists, Alfred Russel Wallace (1823–1913) and Henry Walter Bates (1825–1892)…

Wallace and Bates didn't set out to be famous scientists. Far from it. In fact, Alfred started off as a teacher but he ended up preferring beetles to pupils. I wonder why? At school, young Alfred's favourite subject was biology. (By the way, he hated horrible geography. So it was strange that he spent most of his life travelling around the world.) Later, he read a book about botany that changed his life. From then on, he spent all his spare time wandering about the countryside, studying and sketching plants. He even made his own pressed flower collection. Very pretty. No wonder his brother called him a weed. But green-fingered Alfred didn't care. Whatever anybody else might think, he knew that greens were good for him.

Alfred might have stuck to pressing flowers for the rest of his life. But by chance he met Henry Walter Bates in his local library. Henry was a part-time entomologist, but studying insects didn't pay very well. So he earned his living working in a local brewery. In the morning, he swept the brewery floors. After lunch, he looked for beetles. The two men soon became firm friends and before very long weedy Alfred was well and truly bitten by the beetle bug. But collecting beetles

214

in Britain was dead boring. There just weren't enough new ones around. It was time for curious Wallace and Bates to spread their butterfly net a bit wider. They'd read about the Amazon rainforest in another library book which called it "the garden of the world". And where better to hunt for brand-new beetles than in a truly gigantic garden? They decided to take a tropical trip to the awesome Amazon. It was horribly exciting.

Wallace and Bates arrived in Belem, Brazil in May 1848, on board a cargo ship called *Mischief* after a journey lasting a month. Both men stood blinking in the bright tropical sunshine. Neither of them looked like an intrepid explorer at all. Alfred was pale, gangly and horribly short-sighted. Henry was tall, thin and painfully shy. But looks aren't everything. Without even stopping for a well-earned rest, the two men stocked up with supplies, hired some local guides and a canoe and set off into the jungle. Despite the heat, the flies and the damp, it was like a dream come true. Here's how Alfred described his first sight of the forest:

"I could only marvel at the sombre shades, scarce illuminated by a single direct ray of the sun, the enormous size and height of the trees ... the extraordinary creepers which wind around them, hanging in long festoons from branch to branch."

What's more, it was like being in insect heaven. They'd never seen anything like it before. There were beetles and butterflies everywhere. Wallace and Bates were soon busily beetling away, collecting insect specimens which they pickled or pinned on to cards. Their plan was to ship them back to England where a museum had promised to pay them threepence a piece. Which might not sound much until you know that Henry alone collected 14,712 different types of insects (8,000 of which scientists had never seen before – they got horribly excited)! So he really earned his money. Every day, Henry worked from 9 a.m. to 2 p.m., with a short break for lunch. Here's how he described a typical day in a letter to his brother:

Over my left shoulder slings my double-barrelled gun. In my right hand I take my net; on my left side is suspended a leather bag with two pockets, one for my insect box, the other for powder and two sorts of shot. On my right hand hangs my "game bag", an ornamental affair, with red leather trappings and thongs to hang lizards, snakes, frogs, or large birds. One small pocket in this bag contains papers for wrapping up delicate birds. To my shirt is pinned my pin cushion with six sizes of pins.

But this trip was to be no picnic. On their jungle travels, Alfred and Henry were driven mad by mosquitoes, shot at by unfriendly locals and laid low by life-threatening fevers. Once, a whopping anaconda snake attacked their canoe. It bored a hole in their chicken coop (they'd brought the chickens along for food) with its head and made off with a couple of chickens.

But worse was to come. In August 1852, Alfred decided he'd seen enough of the rainforest for now and set sail for home. Halfway into the voyage, disaster struck. The ship he was sailing in burst into flames and sank, taking Alfred's precious collection of specimens down with it. All poor Alfred's diaries and sketches were lost, apart from some notes about palm trees and some drawings of fish. Alfred himself only just made it back alive. He was finally rescued after spending two weeks adrift at sea.

It was a serious setback. Devastated and broke, Alfred returned to England but he didn't stop his life's work. It wasn't long before he was back among his beloved beetles, this time in South-East Asia. In just eight short years, he collected a staggering 125,000 specimens, including beetles, butterflies and birds. What happened to Henry, you might ask? Well, he spent several more years in the Amazon before heading home to write a book. OK, so it was boringly called *A Naturalist on the River Amazon* but it was so horribly gripping and exciting it became a bestseller. So, for the first time ever, Wallace and Bates put rainforests (and their weird and wonderful wildlife) well and truly on the map. Which was great news for budding geographers everywhere.

How not to get eaten alive
Brave Wallace and Bates lived to tell the tale but other rainforest creatures aren't so lucky. Many jungle animals scoff plants for their tea. So it's a good job there's so much greenery. But some vicious creatures have more sinister eating habits. Forget fruit and veg. Their favourite meals are ... each other! Amazingly, some cunning creatures manage to get away and even turn the tables on their attackers. So if you don't want to end up as elevenses, how on Earth do you do it? If you want to find out how jungle animals stay alive, why not take a peek at this essential Survival Manual. It's been put together by an old friend of Fern's, Major Ray N Forest and it's full of sneaky survival tactics.

SURVIVAL MANUAL

Chameleon

OK, so this is a tough one. But to all you chameleons out there, let's hope you've got plenty of colours in your paintbox because you're going to need them. I know you're normally green and brown but all  that's got to change! Do you hear me? I'm not talking a bit of fawn here, or beige there. I WANT TO SEE CAMOUFLAGE! And I want to see it fast. Yes, in a matter of minutes, you need to change colour to blend in with whatever background you're up against. That way, your enemies won't know where to find you. But you've gotta be ready for action. I mean, this ain't no game of painting by numbers!

Arrow-poison frog

Now, my little friend, just because you're small doesn't mean you don't have to bother. I know you like wearing bright colours on your skin and, granted, they're good for warning your enemies off. I mean, they're really LOUD! But you need more than that. I'm talking poison. I want your slimy skin to ooze deadly juices. Those dudes ain't gonna touch you again, once they get a skinful of that! There's just one problem. Some human hunters might try to roast you over a fire. Don't panic, they don't want to eat you. They want to sweat the poison out of you so they can make poison arrows.

Orchid mantis

You don't fool me. I know you look like a harmless flower but you're a tricky customer all right. I don't think you need me to teach you anything in the way of self protection. Even your wings sway in the breeze just like delicate petals. Very cunning, I give you that. But I know how deceptive appearances can be. Any insect that lands on this bloomer is in for a nasty shock. I've seen you in action, and it ain't pretty. Quick as a flash, you grab the insect and bite its head off. A class act if ever I saw one.

Jaguar

I know, I know. You're the fiercest hunter in the rainforest so why should you listen to lil ol' me. But WISE UP, my friend, and don't let pride come before a fall. You need to keep your wits about you. Yeah, I'm talking to you! OK, so you've got a fur coat to die for which hides you among the dappled forest light. But I want you to be careful. When you're sneaking up on prey, take cover in the undergrowth, then pounce. It's the first rule of laying an ambush. Then you're on your own but with claws like yours, no one's gonna try stealing your supper.

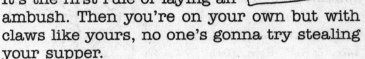

False coral snake

I'm not saying this one's a yellow-belly but when it comes to rainforest survival, you don't have that much to hand. Go on, admit it, you're completely harmless! But fair's fair, give respect where it's due. If this fella can fool everyone into thinking it's poisonous, that's fine by me. You do a pretty good impression of a true coral snake which is deadly poisonous. You've even got the same dashing red, black and yellow colours to warn away the enemy. A brilliant avoidance tactic. (You just have to hope no one sees through your disguise.)

OOPS!

Horrible Health Warning

Eating hairy, poisonous caterpillars is bad for your health. (Even school dinners aren't that dangerous.) At best, you'll break out in an itchy rash. At worse, you might be dead. Here's how the golden potto (a small furry animal like a bushbaby) from Africa gets round this prickly problem. It sniffs out a caterpillar (they smell terrible), then bites it on the head. Then it rubs the ghastly grub between its hands to break off its deadly hairs. It gobbles the caterpillar down then wipes its face clean on a branch.

YUM! YUM!

On the move

If you don't have your own poisonous hairs, you could always try running away. If you can't run fast, you could fly, or glide, or climb the bloomin' trees instead. This is handy for escaping from enemies and for sneaking up on prey. Time to meet some of the niftiest movers in the rainforest...

Animal Olympics

Running Winner: The basilisk lizard can walk on water. It's true. So how on Earth does it do it? Well, it slaps its long, webbed back feet on the water so fast it doesn't fall in. A brilliant way of crossing ponds and rivers if you can't swim!

Climbing Winner: Tiny tree frogs live high up in the rainforest canopy. They've got minute, sticky suction pads on their fingers and toes. The sure-footed frogs can climb straight up a tree  trunk, and even hang upside down from a leaf, without falling off. Bet you don't know anyone who could do that.

 **Flying Winner:** While they're sipping tasty nectar, hummingbirds hover in front of flowers like teeny helicopters. But they have to beat their wings about 90 times a second to stay in the air. That makes the humming sound you can hear. These nifty movers can even fly backwards. Hmmmm…

Swinging Winner: Gibbons are kings of the rainforest swingers. These acrobatic apes hurl themselves through the trees at top speed. Luckily, they've got extra-long  arms with extra-long fingers and toes for grabbing hold of the branches and they can cover 10 metres in a single bound. To match this, you'd have to swing right across your classroom. Now mind where you land.

 **Gliding Winner:** The handsome paradise flying snake can't really fly but it does the next best thing. It glides through the air at high speed. But it doesn't have wings. Instead it launches itself from a tree, then flattens out its body. It floats down to land on a branch like a long, thin parachute.

Could you be a three-toed sloth?

What's green and hairy and hangs around in a tree? No, it isn't your teacher's long-lost woolly cardy.

Give up? The answer is the strange-looking sloth that hangs out in sultry South America. Believe it or not, this appalling animal's even more bone idle than you are. Even the word "sloth" means lazy. Try mentioning that to your mum when she's trying to drag you out of bed. But which of the sloth's filthy habits are too revolting to be true? Try this quick quiz to find out. Mind you don't nod off now...

1 A sloth spends 18 hours a day sleeping. TRUE/FALSE?
2 A sloth's so filthy its fur turns green. TRUE/FALSE?
3 A sloth only comes down to the ground once a week. TRUE/FALSE?
4 Sloths are slower than tortoises. TRUE/FALSE?
5 Scientists who study sloths are always falling asleep. TRUE/FALSE?

Answers:
Believe it or not, they're all TRUE. Sloths really are that bloomin' lazy. Like you, their idea of a perfect day is sleeping, eating, not combing their hair and not having a bath. Yawn! But what's wrong with hanging around in the canopy doing nothing all day? The sleepy sloth doesn't care. Sorry, are we keeping you up? Zzzzz!
1 Even when a sloth isn't asleep, it doesn't shift very far. It

might crawl slowly along a branch, chomping on some leaves. But that's as far as it goes. Awake or asleep, the sloth always hangs upside down in the trees. It holds on with its vice-like claws so it never drops off to sleep, ha! ha! Even its horrible hair hangs upside down so the rain drains off.

2 Normally a sloth has shaggy brown fur but it gets so disgustingly dirty that small plants start sprouting on it. This is what turns it ghastly green. (Actually, this green colouring's horribly useful for hiding the sloth amongst the trees from enemies such as jaguars.) And if that's not horrible enough for you, masses of minute moths crawl about in the sloth's festering fur, munching on the plants.

YUM! LUNCH!

3 Once a week, the sloth leaves its tree … but only to go to the toilet. It has a poo in a hole on the ground then climbs back up again. Meanwhile, the moths fly out of its fur and lay their eggs in the steaming pile of poo. When the grubs hatch, they scoff the sloth poo. Nice! Soon afterwards they turn into adult moths and find a sloth of their own to live on.

4 Even at top speed in the trees, a sloth only crawls along at a sluggish 0.2 kilometres per hour. That's about 20 times slower than you staggering to school. Compared to this slow-coach, tortoises are speedy movers. On the ground, sloths are even slower. Their legs are too weak and feeble to walk very far (it's the lack of exercise) so they drag themselves along on all fours. Strangely, sloths are brilliant at swimming. Not that most sloths ever go near water. In case you were wondering, they do breast-stroke or front crawl.

5 Scientists who study sloths have a tough time keeping their eyes open. I wonder why! Imagine watching a green, furry creature doing nothing for hours on end. It'd be worse than counting sheep. No wonder the first scientists to see a sloth weren't very polite about it. "I have never seen an uglier or more useless creature," one stupefied scientist said.

CAN YOU SPOT THE DIFFERENCE?

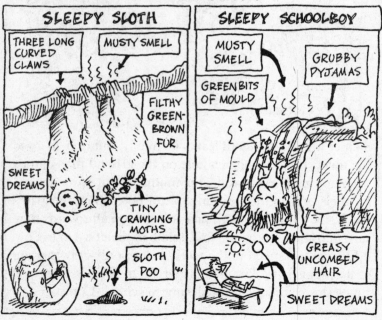

SLEEPY SLOTH

THREE LONG CURVED CLAWS

MUSTY SMELL

FILTHY GREEN-BROWN FUR

SWEET DREAMS

TINY CRAWLING MOTHS

SLOTH POO

SLEEPY SCHOOLBOY

MUSTY SMELL

GRUBBY PYJAMAS

GREEN BITS OF MOULD

GREASY UNCOMBED HAIR

SWEET DREAMS

But before you head off for a good night's kip, WAKEY! WAKEY! Your jungle journey isn't over yet. Far from it. Forget sleepy sloths and plate-sized spiders. Someone else is waiting to meet you in the next chapter. Someone who could teach you a thing or two. (And no, it's not a geography teacher.) But make sure you mind your Ps and Qs with these rainforest residents...

JUNGLE LIVING

Despite the weird wildlife and the wet weather, about 1.5 million people live in the bloomin' rainforests. And they've lived there for thousands of years. They rely on the forest for everything – their food, clothes, homes and medicines. You name it, it's found in the forest somewhere. In return, they treat the rainforest with great respect, making sure they don't do it any harm. Sounds like a great way to live, you might say. But don't be fooled into thinking it's easy. Rainforest living can be horribly hard. I mean, when you're feeling peckish, what do you do? Drag yourself out of your armchair and chomp on a bag of crisps? You definitely *don't* have to set off into the forest to search for something to eat. Think you could hack some real jungle living? Ready to find out how rainforest people really survive? Who better to ask than the Yanomami people of South America. They know the rainforest like the backs of their hands...

My rainforest life by Yarima

My house and family

Hello, my name is Yarima. I live in the rainforest in Brazil, South America. I'm ten years old and I'm a Yanomami. That's what my people are called. My family lives in a village called Toototobi which is quite close to the river. It's a beautiful place to live. All the people in my village live together in a huge house built in a clearing in the forest. There are about a hundred of us in all. The house is called a yano and it's built in the shape of a giant circle. Our yano's made of wood from rainforest trees and it's got a thatched roof made from palm leaves. It's cool in the day and warm at night. Perfect! My dad and the other men in the village built this yano a few years ago. Inside, each of the families has its own fireplace. We hang our hammocks around the fire and that's where we sleep. The fire keeps us warm at night and keeps the mosquitoes away. It's also where we do our cooking. My pet monkey likes to curl up in my hammock with me. I've also got a pet toucan and lots of dogs. I'm

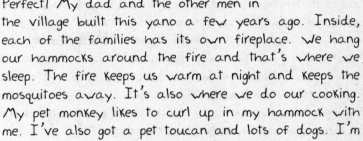

really lucky. In the middle of the yano, there's a big space that's open to the sky. That's where we play and have meetings and parties. I love living in the yano. Apart from my mum, dad and brothers, my grandparents, aunts, uncles and cousins all live there, too. So we're one great big family. There's always someone to talk to or play with or look after you when you're ill. OK, so we fall out and squabble sometimes but we never get bored or lonely.

My day

I get up early in the morning, as soon as the sun comes up. Then I go to the river with the other girls to wash. It's fun splashing each other and diving in. Then we go home and have breakfast. It's usually manioc bread* dipped in pepper sauce or an avocado. After breakfast, we go to school in the yano to learn to read and write. We learn our own Yanomami language and also Portuguese so we can talk to people who live outside the forest. School only lasts for a few hours so it's not too bad. Afterwards we go swimming in the river or climb the trees. Then we have to help our mothers with the chores.

My brothers and the other boys go off with the men to learn how to hunt in the forest. Sometimes they're away for several days, camping in the forest. The men catch monkeys, wild pigs, armadillos and tapirs with their bows and arrows. Sometimes they go fishing in the river. They stand in a canoe and catch fish with their spears. It's very difficult. The boys watch and practise hunting lizards. My brother can't wait to grow up and go hunting for real, even though it can be horribly dangerous. Last week, my uncle was badly hurt when a wild pig charged at him. And sometimes they don't catch anything, which is very bad news for us and we get very hungry.

Yanomami girls like me don't go hunting. I help my mother collect firewood and water. It's very hard work! I also help look after our little garden where we grow manioc, bananas, peanuts and peppers. Sometimes my mum and I go into the forest to collect Brazil nuts, caterpillars and peach palms. And I'm learning to make my own hammock. But it's taking a long time.

My mum and dad are brilliant! They teach us about the forest and about the animals and plants that live there. We learn which plants are good to eat and which can make us ill. They teach us to love the forest because it gives us everything we need to live. My dad says, "Each time you cut down a tree you must ask its forgiveness or a star will fall out of the sky." We also learn to be generous and share what we have with other people. That's very important to the Yanomami people.

I've been feeling very sad lately because my mum's been really ill. She feels very tired and has a fever. All she wants to do is sleep.

My dad says she has the flu – that's a sickness brought to the forest by the goldminers. My dad says people sometimes die of flu and Mum needs special strong medicine. But we don't have any of that. I don't want my mum to die.

A great feast

In the evening, the men come back from the forest and share out the food they've caught. Sometimes we sit around the fire after dinner, telling stories about the forest. Sometimes we have a big party to celebrate a good day's hunting. There's singing, dancing and a huge feast. People come from the villages all around to join in the fun. It's a really exciting time for our village. My friend Marta and I get ready by painting our faces and bodies red and black with coloured dyes made from plant juice. We wear bright green and yellow parrot feathers in our ears. There's loads of delicious food to eat. But the best news is that my mum's feeling loads better and after the feast tonight, my mum and the other women started singing songs about the forest. My friends and I love joining in. We sing songs to thank the forest spirits for giving us enough to eat. We believe that the spirits live in every forest plant and animal. If we make them angry, they can make us ill or take the animals away so we don't have any food. So we have to keep them happy!

The party goes on until late at night but my mum says I've got to go to bed. Tomorrow there's going to be a big meeting in the yano to talk about the illness Mum had. Dad says we've got to do something to stop the goldminers making us sick and harming the forest. I hope we don't have to leave the forest. I love my home.

Come on, monkey, time for bed. Goodnight, everyone.

Manioc's a vegetable a bit like a potato. Rainforest people make it into bread and beer. But first they have to pound it into a pulp and squeeze the juices out. Otherwise it's horribly poisonous. If you ate it raw, you'd have had your chips and that's for sure!

Teacher teaser

Feeling brave? If you want to see your teacher turn crimson with rage, crush up some seeds from the urucu plant, mix them with water and use the paste to paint your face.

But why is your teacher seeing red?

Answer: Because she's just seen your ugly mug, that's why. You see, the urucu paste turns your skin bright red. The Wai Wai people of South America deliberately paint their faces with it to avoid being ambushed by evil spirits. The Wai Wai don't think spirits can see red. So what's your excuse? The Wai Wai also paint their pet dogs red so the sinister spirits can't spot them either. Besides, the pungent paste's great for keeping mosquitoes away.

Fruits of the forest

If you're going to live like a rainforest local, you'd better get used to the food. You might think school dinners taste disgusting. And, of course, you'd be right. But be warned. Forget soggy cabbage and lumpy custard. Check out this revolting rainforest restaurant instead. Some of the dishes on the menu might leave you feeling a teeny bit green. Are you ready to order? Go on, tuck in.

Revolting Rainforest Menu

STARTERS

- **Freshly boiled grasshopper garnished with ants.**
  Make sure you cook the ants for at least six minutes to get all the poison out.
- **Roasted palm grubs on sticks.**
  Eat the grubs whole or split them open and suck out their juicy insides.
- **Delicious hot fruit soup.**
  Made from freshly picked forest fruits, such as soursop, rambutan and durian (despite their strong smell, you can eat the lot), simmered in herb-flavoured water. Pick out anything that looks like small oranges — they're deadly poisonous strychnine fruits.

MAIN COURSE

- **Chef's special rainforest stew.**
  Made from fresh cuts of monkey, tapir and wild pig, and perhaps a bat or two. Boiled until it's soft and tender to chew.
- **Succulent capybara steaks with barbecued banana.**
  Not suitable for guinea pig owners. Capybaras are huge rodents that look like gigantic guinea pigs. They taste like a cross between pork and fish. Apparently.
- **Freshly caught piranha fish.**
  Mind your fingers on their nasty sharp teeth. Served with a side dish of roasted tarantula.

235

- **Slice of fresh honeycomb.**
  Tastes delicious but is horribly risky to collect. First you have to climb a tall tree and stick your hand into a bees' nest. You'll have a bunch of smoking leaves to fend the bees off but chances are you'll still get stung.

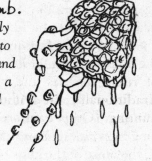

Could you be a rainforest hunter?

If you're hiking through the forest and your stomach starts rumbling, what on Earth can you do? You can't just pop along to the shops. There aren't any shops to pop along to! Feeling brave? You'll need to be. You're about to go hunting for your supper. What do you mean you've gone off your food? Don't worry, you'll be in good company. The Mbuti people of Africa are expert hunters. Stick with them and they'll show you what to do...

1 You pitch camp in the forest. The Mbuti are nomads. This means they move from place to place in search of food. They don't stay anywhere long, just until supplies run out. So they don't need especially hard-wearing homes. Instead, they put up small, round huts

WHERE'S THE TENT? WHERE'S THE SLEEPING BAGS?

made from bent-over branches and leaves. Just right for keeping the rain out. And they're handy because they only take two hours to build.

2 Next day, you wake up at dawn. You light a fire to honour the forest and ask for its blessing on the hunt. After breakfast of roast bananas and rice, you set off into the forest. Traditionally, the Mbuti use large nets and spears for hunting. (Other rainforest locals use bows and arrows, or long blowpipes instead. Today, some use shotguns. Trouble is, the noise of the guns being fired scares the animals away.) The nets are made from super-strong forest vines and can last for years and years.

3 You follow an antelope's tracks through the forest. (The Mbuti also hunt monkeys, snakes and wild pigs.) The Mbuti are expert animal trackers. They know exactly where to go. But ssshhh! You don't want to frighten the animals off or let them know you're coming. So you'll have to walk on tiptoe over the dry, crunchy leaves. The Mbuti can do this without making a sound. Question is, can you?

4 Just then, you spot a group of antelopes grazing among the trees. But don't say anything, whatever you do, or you'll scare them away. Instead, you'll have to make a special hand signal to tell the others what you have seen.

WHAT'S THE HAND SIGNAL FOR ANTELOPE?

5 You hold out your net with the other hunters to make a big semicircle shape. Meanwhile, some of the villagers hide among the surrounding trees. Then suddenly they rush forward and shoo the antelopes into the nets. The hunters kill the antelopes with their spears which they've dipped in deadly poison.

6 You carry the antelopes back to the camp and cook them over the camp-fire. Everyone gets a share of the roast meat. There are baskets of freakily-named forest mushrooms to go with it. Everyone enjoys a feast. Afterwards, you sing and dance around the camp-fire to thank the forest for giving you a good day's hunting.

Mary Kingsley's fang-tastic adventure or "One For The Pot"

But head–hunters weren't the only hazard you'd have faced in the past. Losing your head was one thing, but what about ending up in a cannibal's cooking pot? What a horrible thought. Mind you, this didn't stop plucky English explorer, Mary Henrietta Kingsley (1862–1900). You could say brave Mary stepped out of the frying pan straight into the fire...

Mary had a miserable childhood. Her dad was often away from home and her mum was always ill and Mary had to look after her. When Mary was 30 years old, both her mum and dad died. With nothing to keep her at home anymore, daring Mary decided to set off for Africa to study how the local people lived. Her friends thought she was barmy. For a start, she'd never been to Africa. In fact, she'd never been abroad before. Besides, at that time, travelling alone in a strange country wasn't a very ladylike thing to do. Did Mary care? Did she, heck. She spent a happy year exploring in Africa and if anyone asked her why she was there she had a brilliant excuse. She said she was searching for her long–lost husband and, luckily, it did the trick. But that was just the start of Mary's adventures. The following year she was off again.

The British Museum in London asked her to collect some specimens of rare river fish that were only found in Africa. There was just one teeny problem. The bits of Africa the fish were found in lay deep in the bloomin' rainforest and were horribly risky to reach. So risky that no outsiders had ever been there before. What's more, they were home to some particularly fierce and unfriendly cannibals, alarmingly called the Fang. Most people would have said no, fang-you, and told the museum to find their own bloomin' fish. But Mary was much more daring.

Did Mary live to tell the tale? Or did she end up in very hot water? Here's what one of her letters home might have looked like.

The Ogowe River, Gabon, Africa
July 1895

My dear brother, Charles,

I hope this letter reaches you safely. I'm sorry I haven't written for a while but I've been rather busy, you see. And what a week it has been. You know I'm here collecting fish for the museum? Well, I headed off down the Ogowe in search of some really rare specimens. The first part of the journey was brilliant. I caught a paddle-steamer which was most pleasant and comfortable, I must say. Trouble was, it couldn't go over the rapids so I had to change ships and go on by canoe. What a palaver. We capsized a couple of times and once a crocodile tried to climb on board. (I gave it a good whack on the nose with a paddle and it didn't bother us again.) The leeches are far worse, though. What loathsome creatures they are. Once they get a grip on you, there's no shaking them off. Luckily, I'd packed a pair of your old trousers so I popped them on under my skirt. That made my legs nice and leech-proof, at least.

Anyway, I hired five local men as guides and soon we reached the Great Forest between the Ogowe and Rembwe rivers. That's the jungle to you and me. It was so exciting to be here at last after reading about it in books. Do you know, I'm the first outsider ever to come here? Isn't that exciting? Eventually we reached a Fang village called Efoua where I was lucky enough to find a room. Now, Charles, I know what you're thinking, dear. The Fang are fearsome cannibals who eat intruders for breakfast and I was bound to end up in the cooking pot. But, you know, they've been very good to me so far. I paid my way with some cloth and fish hooks and I've never been frightened at all. Besides, you know my favourite motto, "Never lose your head".

Mind you, yesterday I got the shock of my life. There was a very odd smell in my hut, sort of sweet and sickly like rotten fish. I sniffed around a bit and it seemed to be coming from an old cloth bag hanging on a hook on the wall. What a stink! I'm afraid to say my curiosity got the better of me and I opened the bag and emptied it into my hat. I made sure no one was watching, first. I didn't want to offend them.

241

Anyway, you'll never believe what was in it – a human hand, three big toes, four eyes and two ears! Yes, dear, ears! The hand actually looked quite fresh. I later learned that, even though the Fang are rather partial to eating people, as you feared, they always keep a bit of their victims as a souvenir. It's rather gruesome, I admit, but fascinating, don't you think? But Charles, please don't worry about me. I'm still in one piece. Besides, I've got my little revolver tucked in my boot in case things turn nasty.

We're off to another Fang village tomorrow, though the guides aren't very keen. They're convinced they're going to be boiled alive. We shall see. Then I'm off to climb Mungo Mah Lobel (Mt Cameroon). I've never climbed a mountain before, it's really exciting. But I should be back in good time for Christmas, dear.

Your loving sister,
Mary

PS By the way, I collected 65 brand-new types of fish. Brilliant, isn't it?

BRILLIANT

Mary returned to England in December and immediately became a star. She wrote a best-selling book about her travels and was invited to give lectures and talks to geographical societies. She even had three of the fish she'd found named after her. But her story has a very sad ending. In 1899 she went to South Africa to nurse wounded soldiers and died the following year.

Local people have lived in the rainforest for thousands of years. But today their lives are changing. The forest is being chopped down around them and they're being forced to leave their homes. Many have died from diseases such as malaria, measles and flu. These are brought in by people who come to settle in the forest from outside. Some local people are trying to fight back and protect the forest. Otherwise their ancient way of life may die out. And that would be a terrible tragedy.

Some people have horribly itchy feet. But it's got nothing to do with wearing the same smelly socks for days. Truth is, they simply can't sit still. Take intrepid explorers, for example. You wouldn't catch them sitting around all day, glued to the telly. No, they were always setting off for far-flung places where no outsiders had set foot before. Perilous places like deadly deserts and terrifying mountain peaks. Oh, and bloomin' rainforests, of course. So why on Earth did they do it and why do they still set off today? Some wanted to trade in forest treasures such as spices, timber or gold. They were in it for the money. But others were horrible scientists and geographers. They simply wanted to see the world. And their curiosity made them do strange and unexpected things...

Rambles through the Amazon rainforest

Posh German geographer, Alexander von Humboldt (1769–1859), hated school. He wanted to see the world. But to please his mum, he went off to university and got a dead boring job in the Department of Mines. He spent most of the day deep underground, but at night he headed off into the countryside. You see, Alexander was potty about plants.

In 1796, Alexander's mum died. So he set off on his travels. He resigned from his job and learned map-reading in case he ever got lost. Then he teamed up with top French botanist, Aime Bonpland (1773–1858). Aime trained as a doctor but he much preferred plants to his human patients. Does that make him "barking" mad? Anyway, the two men got on like a house on fire and soon became firm friends. They signed up on a five-year expedition to explore the South Pole where their knowledge of science might come in useful. But at the last minute the trip was called off. Bitterly disappointed, Aime and Alexander walked from France to Spain instead. And there their luck changed. By chance, they met the King of Spain who gave them permission to visit South America. (At that time, South America was ruled by Spain and you needed the king's say-so to go there.) For our heroes, it was like a dream come true. In the South American rainforests, they could study plants to their hearts' content. But it wasn't going to be easy…

Where better to read about their amazing voyage than in these extracts from Alexander's jungle journal? His real journal was much, much longer than this because Alexander made notes about everything – but you get the idea. And he was always amazingly chirpy and cheerful, even when things went horribly wrong.

My Jungle Journal (short version)
by
Alexander Friedrich Wilhelm Heinrich Humbolt. (Baron)

July 1799, Cumana, Venezuela
We sailed from Spain on 5 June. I couldn't believe it. We were off at last! Yippee! Hooray! Look out, world, here I come! I'm so excited, I could burst. The voyage was really brilliant. We spent a few days in Tenerife and climbed an (extinct) volcano. Fantastic. Then the journey proper began. On the way, I took lots of samples of sea water and algae (tiny plants). Then disaster struck. Half the ship's crew went down with typhoid, a dreadful disease. We headed for the nearest port – Cumana in Venezuela (in South America) which is where we are now. Still, every cloud's got a silver lining. Of course, it's terrible for the sick men and I hope they get better but what a bloomin' ace place this is! There's so much to see and do. I don't know where to begin. Trees with monster-sized leaves and huge flowers, and animals and birds everywhere. Heaven!

February 1800, Caracas, Venezuela
We've been here since November. It's the rainy season, you see, so it's far too wet to travel. But there's no time to get bored. We've been sorting out all the specimens we've collected so

far – there's hundreds of them! Once the weather turns drier, we'll travel south to the Orinoco River. Apparently, there's a stream called the Casiquiare linking it to the mighty Amazon. I can't wait.

March 1800, almost at the Orinoco River, Venezuela
What a month! We set off from Caracas on horseback with our trusty local guides. But riding across the river plains was hell. Even I found it hard to keep smiling. We thought we'd suffocate in the baking heat, die of thirst or be eaten alive by bugs. Still, mustn't complain. We've reached the rainforest at last, in good health and good spirits considering what we've been through. We travel all day, then pitch camp on the riverbank. We hang our hammocks in the trees around a blazing fire. Lovely!

The guides catch fish for supper while Bonpland and I write our diaries up. It's really rather cosy. The fire also helps keep jaguars at bay. You can hear them roaring away in the dark. Scared? Not me. Jaguars are just big pussy cats! Aaaaghhh! What on Earth was that?

1 April, 1800, the Orinoco River

We've swapped our horses for a canoe and we're paddling up the Orinoco. Into the unknown. What a thrill! But it's bloomin' hot, I can tell you. Luckily, our canoe's got a little thatched hut at the back to keep the sun off. It's stuffed full of plants and animal cages (mostly full of parrots and monkeys) so it's a bit of a squash if we get in. Tra! la! la! la! Tra! la! la! la! Messing about on the river...

4 April, 1800, further up the Orinoco

Phew! What a narrow squeak. We stopped near a thick patch of jungle. I was bursting to go off and explore. What a place! What plants! What animals! What a paradise on Earth! Ahem. Sorry, got carried away. Anyway, I stopped to investigate a freaky fungus on the forest floor, and then I looked up ... straight at a jaguar! Shivers ran down my spine. What on Earth was I to do? Then I remembered a useful piece of advice that someone once gave me: "Should you meet a jaguar, just turn slowly and walk away. But don't look back."

And that's exactly what I did. Very slowly, I turned my back and walked away. At any moment, I expected the creature to pounce. Then I'd have been a goner. Luckily for me, when I dared turn round, the jaguar had disappeared. It must have eaten already.

PS I take back what I said about pussy cats.

May 1800, the Casiquiare River

At last, we've found the Casiquiare. And not a moment too soon. It's been pretty hard going, even for me. Crossing the rapids in a flimsy canoe was frightening enough. But what really bugged us was the mosquitoes. We slapped on rancid alligator fat to keep those irritating insects off. It smelt terrible and it didn't do much good. Still, I'm trying to stay cheerful, despite it all. Poor Bonpland's not quite so chirpy. He's been bitten all over, and his face is all puffed up and covered in blisters. Oh, and we're down to eating our last few ants and some dried cocoa beans. I suppose it's better than nothing.

A few days later, Esmeralda

Funny how such a terrible place can have such a pretty name. Still it hasn't been a complete waste of time. I've conducted a very exciting experiment. The local people told me they use a deadly poison called curare to tip their hunting arrows. It's made from the bark of a jungle vine. And it can kill a monkey (or human) in minutes. But it's only fatal if it enters your bloodstream. Apparently. Well, you know me, I love a challenge. So I swallowed some to see. OK, it was risky but guess what? I'm still here! Luckily.

To cut a seriously long story short...
Alex didn't have to wait long for his next trip. As soon as poor old Bonpland was on his feet, the two were off again. For the next four years, they hacked through rainforests, squelched through swamps and scaled more violent volcanoes. Back home in Europe, they were treated like superstars, particularly Alexander. He had hundreds of places named after him, including a crater on the Moon. Why? Well, no one had ever made such a long journey simply for horrible geography's sake. What's more, Alex's real diaries were crammed with valuable notes and sketches of places, people and wildlife never seen before.

Horrible rainforest holidays
What's the worst holiday you've ever had? The one when you lost your luggage or when it poured with rain? Don't worry. You're in bloomin' good company. The unfortunate travellers you're about to meet have some truly terrible tales to tell about holidays from hell. Would *you* go on holiday with any of this lot? On second thoughts, you might be better off staying at home. Here's Fern to introduce you to them...

NAME: Isabela Godin (1729–1792)
NATIONALITY: Peruvian
HOLIDAY FROM HELL:

French explorer, Jean Godin, thought he'd booked the holiday of a lifetime when he set off down the Amazon in 1749. He was going back to France after years exploring the rainforest. His patient wife, Isabela, stayed behind until he could fetch her. Little did she know, it would be another 20 years before she saw her holidaying husband again. But Isabela wasn't to be put off. She finally grew tired of waiting and set off on her own on one of the worst holidays ever known. One by one, her travelling companions ran away, or drowned, or died from hunger and disease. Soon only plucky Isabela was left. Half-dead, she struggled on alone, eating roots and insects. The food was terrible! Luckily, some friendly locals helped her reach the coast. And guess what? A few weeks later, against the odds, Isabela and Jean were reunited. It might have been a holiday from hell but it had a happy ending!

NAME: Charles Waterton (1782–1865)
NATIONALITY: British
HOLIDAY FROM HELL:

South America is one of the world's most exotic holiday hotspots. As Charles Waterton found out. He made several trips there to find types of jungle animals. Let's just say he enjoyed adventure holidays. He shot the animals and stuffed their skins so that he could study them at leisure. But it was horribly risky work. Dare-devil Charles once captured a boa constrictor alive by wrestling it to the ground and tying its jaws up with his braces. He also rode on the back of a giant alligator, using its front legs as reins. Back home, he set up a nature reserve to put all his weird wildlife and holiday mementoes in.

NAME: Richard Spruce (1817–1893)
NATIONALITY: British
HOLIDAY FROM HELL:

Top botanist Richard Spruce enjoyed the sort of holiday where you plan your own itinerary. He spent years collecting thousands of new types of Amazon plants, mapped miles of rivers and learned to speak 21 local languages. So he didn't need a holiday rep to help him do his souvenir shopping. But it wasn't all plain sailing. Several times, Richard nearly died from malaria. Another time he woke up to hear his guides plotting to kill him in his sleep. Luckily, he managed to talk them out of it, proving that it was a good idea to learn a little of the local languages. It's always appreciated.

NAME: Benedict Allen (born 1960)
NATIONALITY: British
HOLIDAY FROM HELL:

There are some holidays that only the most adventurous traveller should dare to take on. Benedict Allen was just such a holidaymaker. In the 1980s, he spent months in the Amazon rainforest, travelling by foot and dug-out canoe. No luxury air-conditioned coach for this intrepid explorer. The trouble started when his local guides left him and he lost his canoe. For a month, he struggled alone, eating only dried soup, fried locusts, nuts and ... dog! Yep, he finally had to kill and eat his pet dog. But, despite nearly dying from a fever, plucky Benedict made it out alive. We say: well done, Benedict, for being our bravest holidaymaker so far!

Could you be a budding explorer?

Just imagine if you were lost in the rainforest. How on Earth would you survive? Would you know how to shake off a poisonous snake or make friends with a blood-sucking leech? Try this life or death survival quiz to find out how you'd do. But be careful. With all the horrible hazards about, it's a bloomin' miracle anyone gets out alive. What's that? You'd rather do extra homework than risk your neck in there? Must be bad. You'd better send your geography teacher to the rainforest instead. And don't let him peek at the answers...

1 You're in the steamy rainforest and you're dying for a drink. Trouble is, there's very little water around, despite all the rain. Which plant can help you quench your thirst?

a) A vine.

b) A bromeliad.

c) A pitcher plant.

2 It's night-time and you're nodding off to sleep. Then something large, black and SCARY flaps by. It's a vampire bat and it's after your blood. How do you avoid being bitten?

a) Snore very loudly. It'll scare the bat off.

b) Stop watching so many late-night horror films. Vampires aren't real, silly.

c) Wrap yourself up in a mosquito net, even if there aren't any mosquitoes around.

3 Help! Another blood-sucker's taking a liking to you. This time it's a loathsome leech. Talk about making your skin crawl! If a leech sucks up to you and sinks its jaws into your leg, how on Earth do you get rid of it?

a) Pull it off.

b) Wait till it's full of blood, then it'll drop off.

c) Sprinkle salt on it.

4 Watch your step. There's a gigantic log blocking your way. At least, it looks like a log, but is it? In the rainforest, things aren't always as harmless as they seem. Remember the murderous orchid mantis? Just in case the log's *actually* a poisonous snake, what should you do? After all, you don't want to put your foot in it, do you?

a) Step on it … gently.

b) Pick it up and throw it away.

c) Poke it with a stick.

5 You've been walking for miles. You're all hot and bothered and you feel as if you're about to faint. You're not sure you can go any further. What should you eat to make you feel better?

a) A banana.

b) Some salt.

c) A chocolate bar.

Answers:

1 a), b) and **c)**. All three would do the trick. But be careful. If you're getting water from a vine, make sure you choose the right one. Some vines are horribly poisonous. Here's how you can tell. Cut the vine with a knife. If the liquid that pours out is clear and doesn't burn your mouth, it's perfectly safe to drink. If it's cloudy, red or yellowish and stings, steer clear. Make sure you strain water from bromeliads or pitcher plants first to get rid of the creepy-crawlies.

2 c) The bats can't nibble you through the net. Phew! But keep your nose, fingers and toes safely tucked inside. These are the bits beastly bats love best. Whatever you do, try not to snore. It tells the bloomin' bats where to find you. Vicious vampire bats attack their victims at night while they're sleeping. Apart from snoring humans, they also attack cows, horses and pigs. They nip your skin with their razor-sharp teeth, then lap up your blood. The strange thing is you won't feel a thing because their spit numbs the pain. Then the bloated bats return to their roost and sick up some of the blood for their batty relations. Vile.

3 b) and c). Leeches live on the damp forest floor. Like vampire bats, they feed on blood. They sink their teeth into your skin, then slurp until they're full.

Don't try to pull a blood-sucking leech off, whatever you do. They've got sticky suckers at either end and they'll cling on for dear life. Wait until their vile bodies are full of blood, then they'll simply drop off. (This may take some time – a thirsty leech can slurp five times its own weight in blood. IN ONE SITTING!) Or sprinkle them with salt or sugar. This'll make them shrivel up and die. You have to be cruel to be kind. Better still, tuck your trousers into your socks and wear a pair of long socks on top. It won't look very cool but the leeches will loathe it!

4 a) Step on the log, *very* gently. If it ups sticks and slithers off, it's probably a snake. Never ever poke a snake with a stick. If you want to stay alive. Some deadly poisonous snakes lurk on the rainforest floor. And they're horribly hard to spot. Some look exactly like fallen logs or piles of leaves.

But don't be fooled. Mess with one of these beauties and you'll be sorry. Dead sorry. Take the bushmaster snake, for instance. If a bushmaster bites you, you'll be dead in hours. First you start sweating and throwing up, then you get a splitting headache. Eventually you lose consciousness. Your only hope is to get yourself along to a doctor fast.

5 b) You'll sweat buckets in the rainforest because it's so bloomin' steamy and hot. Trouble is, sweat's mainly made from water and salt, and you need both to stay alive. Lose too much of either and you'll feel feverish and weak. Then you'll feel dizzy and tired, and eventually, you'll get delirious and die. A very nasty way to go. The best thing to do is dissolve some salt in water and sip this, slowly. You might fancy a nourishing banana later, when you're feeling better. But forget the chocolate – it'll melt in the heat. Rainforest people keep cool by not wearing much but you (or your teacher) should cover up well. Long sleeves and trousers will stop you getting badly bitten and scratched.

I'VE GOT A SPARE HAT IF YOU NEED IT?

Now add up your teacher's score...
Feeling generous? Award your teacher 10 points for each right answer.

Score: 0–20. Oh dear! Your teacher won't last long in the rotten rainforest. He's just too bloomin' green. At this rate, he'd be eaten alive before you could say "Watch out, there's a crocodile!" Wouldn't that be a pity?

Score: 30–40. Your teacher's got what it takes to be a budding explorer if he keeps his wits about him. But hang on... What are those two little bite marks on his neck? Aaaggh! He's been bitten by a blood–sucking bat!

Score: 50. Bloomin' marvellous. Your teacher's survived and he'll be back at school in no time. What's more, he'd make a brilliant rainforest explorer. Compared with teaching you, coping with loathsome leeches and sinister snakes will be easy peasy!

Modern-day exploration

Bored of sitting around all day, playing computer games? As if. Still, if it's a life of adventure you're after, why not head for the rainforest yourself? After all, you don't want your teacher getting big-headed, do you? For years, rainforests had horrible geographers stumped. They were desperate to sneak a peak in the canopy but it was just too bloomin' high up to see. Today, there are lots of ways of travelling through the treetops. Got a good head for heights? You'll need one where you're going...

Modern scientists and geographers head for the rainforests to study the wildlife and find out how the place works. They use ropes and harnesses to climb the tallest trees. They pinched the idea from mountaineers. They fire a fine rope over a branch on the end of an arrow, with a stronger rope tied to the end. They tie it on tightly, then haul themselves up. To get about from tree to tree, they use light metal walkways and ladders over 100 metres above the ground. (You'll soon get used to the swaying.) That's like popping out for an afternoon stroll on top of a 30-storey building. Freaky, or what?

You could also hitch a lift in a hot-air balloon or grab a ride in a cage dangling from the end of a massive crane.

SOFA, SO GOOD

If all this sounds like horribly hard work, you could always haul a comfy armchair up with you. That's what one bone–idle geographer did.

Yikes! Feeling dizzy? Better not look down. Of course, you could always keep your feet on the ground and monitor the rainforest by radar or satellite instead.

Earth-shattering fact

American explorer, Eric Hansen, would have given anything for a ride in a hot-air balloon. In the 1980s, plucky Eric spent months in the jungles of Borneo, visiting places marked "unknown" on the map. Armed with only a bed sheet, a change of clothes and some goods for trading, he travelled by foot and dug-out canoe. So far, so good. But get this. The real trouble started when Eric was mistaken by the locals for a bali saleng, an evil jungle spirit who was thought to kill people and suck their blood. He wasn't one, of course, but he got out of the forest, and he got out of it fast!

The good news is that there's still plenty of bloomin' rainforest left for budding geographers like you to explore. The bad news is it might not be around for long. All over the world, rainforests are being cut down and burned at an alarming rate. So if you're planning a visit, you'd better get your skates on...

FACING THE AXE

Bloomin' rainforests were once a lot bigger than they are today. And I mean *a lot*. They used to cover about a third of the Earth. Today there's less than half of this left. Sad to say, all over the world, precious rainforests are for the chop. So why are rainforests in deadly danger? Who's to blame? The bad news is that *we are* – horrible humans. Truth is, we're putting terrible pressure on the fragile rainforests and the rainforests can't fight back. Once the forests have gone, they can't grow back. Pretty depressing, isn't it? So why on Earth are rainforests going up in smoke? We sent Fern to get to the root of the problem...

Going up in smoke

So what's happening to the bloomin' rainforests, then?

They're being chopped down, that's what. Then some of the trees are burned to a cinder. So thousands of precious plants and animals go up in flames. Then the bulldozers move in...

Oh dear. Is this happening very fast?

Yep, it is. Unfortunately. Horrible geographers don't know exactly how rapidly rainforests are disappearing but it's at a truly alarming rate. Some experts estimate that a patch of forest the size of 60 football pitches is chopped down EVERY MINUTE. That's a chunk the size of Switzerland EVERY YEAR. Put another way, in the time it takes you to read this page, about 40,000 rainforest trees will have gone for good!

At this rate, how long will the rainforests last?

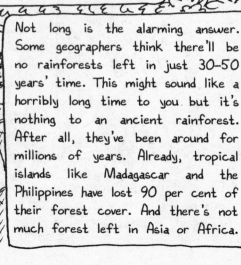

Not long is the alarming answer. Some geographers think there'll be no rainforests left in just 30–50 years' time. This might sound like a horribly long time to you but it's nothing to an ancient rainforest. After all, they've been around for millions of years. Already, tropical islands like Madagascar and the Philippines have lost 90 per cent of their forest cover. And there's not much forest left in Asia or Africa.

So why are rainforests for the chop?

Good question. But guess what? Like most things in geography, there isn't a nice, straightforward answer. Here are some of the worst culprits:

• **Logging.** *About half the rainforest is being chopped down for the timber trade. You see, valuable tropical trees like mahogany are worth thousands and thousands of pounds. The timber's sold to people in rich countries to make posh furniture, doors and windows, loo seats, coffins and chopsticks. Trouble is, the heavy machines used to cut the trees down damage the forest for miles around and hundreds of other trees are wasted.*

• **Gold mining.** *Some rainforests are rich in precious metals and gemstones such as gold, silver and diamonds. And greedy humans can't wait to get rich quick. But the*

chemicals they use to get at the gold are making the rainforest rivers seriously dirty. So fish and plants can't survive. Not to mention rainforest people who rely on the rivers for water and food. And to make matters worse, the miners build roads to take them and their massive machines to work, ruining vast stretches of forest.

• **Farming.** Millions of people are moving out of crowded cities and into the rainforests. They clear plots of land to build houses and grow crops. But rainforest soil is quite thin and poor and the goodness is soon used up. Which means the people have to pack up, move somewhere else and start all over again. Local people have done this for years but they only clear smallish patches of forest. And they leave the land plenty of time to recover in between. But with so many new farmers to cope with, the forest can't take the pressure.

• **Cattle ranching.** Next time you tuck into a tasty hamburger, spare a thought for where the meat came from. Chances are it's from the rainforest far away in South America. Every year, huge stretches of forest are being cleared for beef cattle to graze on. Then the cattle are sold for their meat. Turning the bloomin' rainforest into fast food. Problem is, the grass they graze on sucks the goodness from the soil, leaving it dry and dead. Then the cattle are moved on.

You bet it would. If the rainforests go up in smoke, so do millions of amazing plants and animals. They're killed or lose their homes. Experts think that at least 100 types of animals and plants are being wiped out every single week. And extinction is for ever. Nothing can ever bring them back. Among the animals on the brink is the beautiful Spix's macaw (a macaw's a bigish parrot). There's only one lonely Spix's macaw left in the wild (another 40 live in zoos). Parrots are also captured and sold for pets. It's against the law but it's tricky to stop. Other animals in danger include orangutans, jaguars, birdwing butterflies... Sadly the list goes on and on.

And that's just for starters. Closer to home, here are six other things you wouldn't have if the rainforests went up in smoke. (What d'ya mean, you didn't know they came from the forest in the first place?) Without bloomin' rainforests, you'd miss out on...

1 Brazil nuts Yes, those festive nuts you crunch at Christmas grow on bloomin' rainforest trees. But mind your teeth. They're tremendously tough nuts to crack. They grow in hard shells inside huge pods, as big as cannonballs. You get juicy bananas, pineapples, oranges and lemons from the rainforest too.

2 Chocolate Yummy choccy's made from the beans of the cocoa tree which grows in the rainforest. You know those chocolate coins you get at Christmas? The ones in little glittery string bags? Well, until about 150 years ago, in Mexico, real chocolate beans were used as money.

3 Chewing gum Didn't know that chewing gum grows on trees? Well, it does. It's made from the juice of the rainforest chicle tree. You cut slits in the bark and the sticky goo oozes out. It's boiled up until it goes thick, then shaped into blocks. Tasty mint and fruit flavours are added later.

4 Vanilla ice cream OK, you'd have the ice cream but not the tasty vanilla flavouring. It's made from the sun-dried pods of an exotic rainforest orchid. But vanilla's not the only succulent spice in the rainforest. There's also the pepper you put on food and the ginger in scrummy ginger biscuits.

5 House plants Offer to water your mum's best pot plants, then take a good, long look at them. Chances are some of them are rainforest bloomers. Cheese plants, rubber plants, African violets and nasturtiums might look at home on the mantelpiece but they originally grew wild in the jungle.

6 Cane furniture Cane's used to make baskets, mats and comfy armchairs. But it starts off as a woody rainforest vine. Its real name is rattan but it's also called the "wait-a-while" plant because once it sinks its sharp thorns into you, it takes you a while to break free again. Local people use strips of rattan as toothbrushes but they snap the spines off first.

Miracle medicines

Brazil nut choccies and ice cream might taste scrummy but you could live without them. Honestly! Some other rainforest bloomers could actually save your life. About a quarter of all the medicines we take when we're sick are made with plants that grow in rainforests. And scientists think there's loads more vital, live–saving veg just waiting to be discovered. Veg that could cure killer diseases like cancer and Aids.

Of course, local people have used these marvellous medicines for years. And scientists hope that by finding out more about their usefulness they'll be able to save the rainforests. But could you be a rainforest plant doctor? Look at the list of symptoms below. Then try to pick the correct plant cure. On second thoughts, some of these plants are deadly poisonous except in very small doses. You might kill the patient you're trying to cure. Better leave it to an expert, like our very own Doc Leaf.

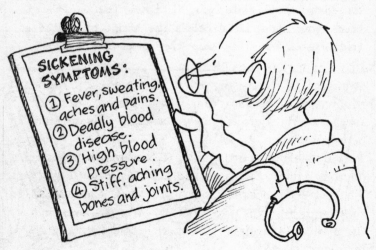

SICKENING SYMPTOMS:
1. Fever, sweating, aches and pains.
2. Deadly blood disease.
3. High blood pressure.
4. Stiff, aching bones and joints.

Answers:

1 b) The bark of the cinchona tree contains a drug called quinine. The bark's stripped off and made into medicine which is used to treat the deadly disease malaria. It's spread by murderous mosquitoes and kills millions of people each year.

2 d) This brilliant little bloomer contains chemicals that doctors can use to treat the killer disease leukaemia. That's a type of cancer of the blood. It's already saved thousands of lives and doctors only discovered it in the 1950s. (Of course, local people had known about it for years.)

3 a) The beans from this rainforest tree can help to lower your blood pressure and treat glaucoma (that's a type of eye disease that can make you go blind). But in Africa, they were traditionally used to decide if a person was guilty. How? Well, if the suspect ate them, and survived, he or she was thought to be innocent. Sounds simple, doesn't it. Trouble is, the beans have a deadly secret. On their own, they're horribly poisonous. So whether or not you were really innocent, you could well end up being dead.

INNOCENT, INNOCENT, INNOCENT, GUILTY...

4 c) A yam looks a bit like a potato but this vital veg isn't used to make lumpy mash. Medicines made from Mexican yams are used for treating painful diseases of the bones and joints like arthritis and rheumatism. However, they have to be prepared very carefully. In large amounts, some yams can be poisonous.

People in peril

You might not think it when your mum's moaning at you for being late for school or you can't do your homework (again) but you're dead lucky. At least when you come home from school, your home's still bloomin' standing! Rainforest people aren't so bloomin' fortunate. They rely on the forest for everything – their homes, food and their livelihoods. And they lose them all when the forest's cut down.

Take the plight of the Penan people. They've lived in the Borneo rainforest for hundreds of years. Traditionally, they wander from place to place in search of animals to hunt and food to gather. They believe the forest is sacred and treat it with great respect. After all, they say, they are part of the forest and the forest is part of them. But today, the forest is being  chopped down for timber and their lives have been turned upside down. Many have been forced to leave the forest and settle in permanent homes far away. For the wandering Penan, it's like being in prison. The Penan people are trying to fight back to save their precious forest. But it's a terrible struggle. When they block the roads to stop the loggers, they're sent to prison or fined. What's more, many are dying from deadly diseases like malaria and flu brought into the forest by loggers. It's a desperate situation. For the Penan and many people like them, the future looks pretty bleak.

Horrible weather warning

Scientists say chopping the rainforests down is making the world's weather worse. How? Well, when the trees go up in flames, they spew tonnes of carbon dioxide gas into the atmosphere. (It also comes from cars and factories.)

This acts like a giant blanket around the Earth. It traps the heat coming from the sun and keeps the Earth snug and warm. Too snug and warm.

If the Earth gets too hot, it could mean stormier weather. And that's not all. It could melt the ice at the perishing poles, making the sea level higher. Then woe betide you if you live near the coast…

HELP!

Fatal floods are another worry. The rainforests act like giant sponges. You know, like that squishy yellow thing you soap yourself with in the bath but on a gigantic scale. The sponge-like trees soak up the rain through their roots and leaves. What's more, their roots bind the fragile rainforest soil together. Chop down the trees and there's nothing to suck up the heavy rain. It floods the land and flows into rivers, making them overflow. Before you know it, you've got a furious, full-blown flood that can wash away whole villages and hillsides. And there's nothing you can do to stop it.

Pretty grim, isn't it? But is it all doom and gloom? Or can the rot really be stopped? Time to find out what's being done to save the bloomin' rainforests...

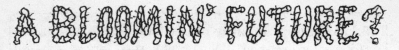

A BLOOMIN' FUTURE?

Unless something's done to save them soon, there won't be any rainforests left. The good news is that conservation groups, governments and local people all over the world are working hard to stop the rot. But saving the rainforest isn't as straightforward as it sounds. Many rainforests grow in poor, overcrowded countries. Thousands of people from chockful cities are forced into the forests to find enough space to live. And rich countries pay them lots of much-needed dosh for timber and other rainforest treasures. It's a horribly tricky business. Here are a few of the things people are trying to do:

1 National parks. These are protected patches of rainforest where logging and mining are banned. In the 1970s, the Kuna people of Panama set up their own reserve to save their traditional culture and the forest wildlife. Scientists or tourists must pay a fee to visit. No one else is allowed in. The Korup National Park in Cameroon, Africa, was set up in the 1980s. It is helping to protect hundreds of rare apes and monkeys and thousands of precious plants. Local people can hunt and fish in a ring of land around the park but not inside the park itself.

2 Planting trees. In many places, local people rely on the rainforests for firewood. They use the wood for cooking and heating. And it's putting the forest under great strain. Planting new trees can't replace the original forest (that takes thousands of years) but it certainly takes the pressure off it. In Brazil, scientists are busy bombing the forest with billions of tropical tree seeds to try to repair the damage. They fly over the forest and drop the seeds inside tiny balls of jelly to protect them as they land. Clever, eh?

3 Horrible holidays. For the holiday of a lifetime, why not check out the rainforest gorillas of Central Africa. They're some of the rarest animals on Earth. You'll need to save up – it's horribly costly – but you'll be doing your bit to keep the rainforests in one piece. Some of your hard-earned cash helps protect the apes' forest home. Some helps the local people. But be warned. You'll be made very welcome, but only as long as you don't leave any litter and you treat the rainforest with respect.

4 Rainforest perfumes. People are looking at ways of using rainforest resources without ruining the forest. Want to do your bit to save the rainforests? And do your Christmas shopping at the same time? Why not treat your mum to a nice big bottle of the gorgeous, the lovely, the delectable … Essence of Rainforest?

ESSENCE of RAINFOREST

The fabulous forest fragrance that will really get right up your nose!

TAKE YOUR PICK FROM OUR BRAND NEW RANGE OF Sensational Forest Scents

OUR GUARANTEE TO YOU

THESE PUNGENT PONGS ARE COLLECTED BY US FROM EXCLUSIVE RAINFOREST BLOOMERS. FLOWERS NO ONE HAS EVER SMELLED BEFORE. THAT'S HOW BLOOMIN' RARE THEY ARE. BUT DON'T WORRY- THE RAINFOREST'S SAFE IN OUR HANDS. WE DON'T EVEN HAVE TO PICK THEM. USING THE LATEST TECHNOLOGY, WE SEAL EACH FLOWER IN A GLASS GLOBE, THEN PUMP ALL THE AIR OUT. INCLUDING THE SMELL.
WITHOUT HARMING A SINGLE PETAL.

279

5 Iguana farming. That's right, iguanas. Iguanas are long lizards that normally lounge about in rainforest trees. But they also make ideal farm animals.

When German geographer Dr Dagmar Werner decided to set up an iguana farm, people thought she was crazy. Why couldn't she stick to boring sheep and cows like everybody else? Well, local people like eating iguana. (Apparently they taste a bit like chicken. Fancy a tasty plate of iguana and chips?) But so much rainforest has been chopped down and so many iguanas hunted, they're becoming rather rare. So Dr Werner rears them on her farm, then releases them into the forest. That way, people have enough to eat and are encouraged to protect the iguanas' tree homes. Ingenious, eh?

Earth-shattering fact

If there isn't a rainforest near where you live, why not grow your own indoors? That's what scientists are doing in Cornwall, England. They've built an enormous greenhouse (as big as four soccer pitches and 60 metres tall) and planted more than 10,000 rare rainforest plants inside, including some huge rubber trees. Visitors can ride around the rainforest on a small train. Why not pop along and take a peak?

A bloomin' future?

The burning question is: will any of these campaigns really work? Or are scientists fighting a losing battle? The truth is, nobody knows for certain. And unfortunately time's running out. Fast! Left alone, bloomin' rainforests might grow back but it'll take thousands of years. And they'll never be quite the same again. Scientists agree that one way to persuade people to save the forests is to teach them how vital and valuable they are. Before it's too bloomin' late. So why not grab a victim … I mean, friend … and bamboozle them with your new-found forest knowledge? Better still, start with your very own geography teacher. Unless she's sneaked back to Planet Blob, of course.

If you're still interested in finding out more, here are some web sites you can visit.

www.rgs.org
The Royal Geographical Society's web site.

www.desertusa.com
This site is about American deserts and is full of scorching facts about the deserts and the plants and wildlife that live in them.

www.nhm.ac.uk/museum/tempexhib/gobi
The Natural History Museum web site has an article about the dinosaurs found in the Gobi Desert.

www.yahooligans.com/around_the_world/countries
The Yahooligans site has articles about many countries around the world.

www.foe.co.uk
The Friends of the Earth UK web site has information about endangered habitats, including rainforests.

www.rainforestfoundationuk.org
Loads of fascinating information about rainforests. Log on to find out how to save your own patch of rainforest.

www.forests.org
The Rainforest Information Centre's web site is packed with facts about rainforests and other types of forests around the world.

www.ran.org
The Rainforest Action Network's web site. The Network works to protect the rainforests and support rainforest people.

www.survival.org.uk
Survival International's web site. Survival is a worldwide organization helping local people to protect their homes and land. Contact them for a copy of their brilliant pack "We, the world". It includes info about the lives of the Yanomami and Ba–aka rainforest people.

Other titles in this series:
Violent Volcanoes
Odious Oceans
Stormy Weather
Raging Rivers
Desperate Deserts
Earth-Shattering Earthquakes
Freaky Peaks
Bloomin' Rainforests
Perishing Poles
Intrepid Explorers
Wild Islands

Two books in one:
Raging Rivers and Odious Oceans
Violent Volcanoes and Earth-Shattering Earthquakes